Samuel French Acting Edition

Gwen and Gwen
A Play in Three Acts

by Nancy Kiefer

SAMUELFRENCH.COM   SAMUELFRENCH.CO.UK

Copyright © 1985, 1986, 1997 by Nancy Kiefer
All Rights Reserved

GWEN AND GWEN is fully protected under the copyright laws of the United States of America, the British Commonwealth, including Canada, and all other countries of the Copyright Union. All rights, including professional and amateur stage productions, recitation, lecturing, public reading, motion picture, radio broadcasting, television and the rights of translation into foreign languages are strictly reserved.

ISBN 978-0-573-63040-8

www.SamuelFrench.com
www.SamuelFrench.co.uk

For Production Enquiries

United States and Canada
Info@SamuelFrench.com
1-866-598-8449

United Kingdom and Europe
Plays@SamuelFrench.co.uk
020-7255-4302

Each title is subject to availability from Samuel French, depending upon country of performance. Please be aware that *GWEN AND GWEN* may not be licensed by Samuel French in your territory. Professional and amateur producers should contact the nearest Samuel French office or licensing partner to verify availability.

CAUTION: Professional and amateur producers are hereby warned that *GWEN AND GWEN* is subject to a licensing fee. Publication of this play(s) does not imply availability for performance. Both amateurs and professionals considering a production are strongly advised to apply to Samuel French before starting rehearsals, advertising, or booking a theatre. A licensing fee must be paid whether the title(s) is presented for charity or gain and whether or not admission is charged. Professional/Stock licensing fees are quoted upon application to Samuel French.

No one shall make any changes in this title(s) for the purpose of production. No part of this book may be reproduced, stored in a retrieval system, or transmitted in any form, by any means, now known or yet to be invented, including mechanical, electronic, photocopying, recording, videotaping, or otherwise, without the prior written permission of the publisher. No one shall upload this title(s), or part of this title(s), to any social media websites.

For all enquiries regarding motion picture, television, and other media rights, please contact Samuel French.

MUSIC USE NOTE

Licensees are solely responsible for obtaining formal written permission from copyright owners to use copyrighted music in the performance of this play and are strongly cautioned to do so. If no such permission is obtained by the licensee, then the licensee must use only original music that the licensee owns and controls. Licensees are solely responsible and liable for all music clearances and shall indemnify the copyright owners of the play(s) and their licensing agent, Samuel French, against any costs, expenses, losses and liabilities arising from the use of music by licensees. Please contact the appropriate music licensing authority in your territory for the rights to any incidental music.

IMPORTANT BILLING AND CREDIT REQUIREMENTS

If you have obtained performance rights to this title, please refer to your licensing agreement for important billing and credit requirements.

GWEN AND GWEN had its world premiere at the Mapleleaf Theatre (at the Grand River Vineyard), Cleveland, Ohio, November, 1988 with the following artists:

ESTELLE REEVES . . . . Diana Tucker

GWEN KESSLER . . . . Susan Pilon

GWEN II . . . . Kathy Yates

MARY ROSE KESSLER . . . . Martha Vail

Stage Direction Steve Ritchey
Lighting Design Lori Diemer
Scenic Design Thom Bowers
Costume Design Jeffrey Ward

CAST OF CHARACTERS

GWEN KESSLER:
A woman in her mid-thirties; plain-looking and poorly dressed.

GWEN II:
The physical opposite of Gwen; stylish, well-dressed and heavily made up.

ESTELLE REEVES:
A social worker in her forties; she is physically nondescript and dresses very professionally.

MARY ROSE KESSLER:
Gwen's mother; a plain, unstylish woman in her late-sixties.

SCENE

The play is set in a dingy, morbid one-room apartment, littered with garbage and debris. The set looks increasingly chaotic as the play progresses.

TIME: The present.

STRUCTURE

ACT I:
    Scene One: The day before Gwen is to be released from the group psychiatric home where she has been living for the past year.
    Scene Two: The next day.

ACT II: A week later

ACT III: A month later

For Jeannie

ACT I

Scene One

(SETTING: GWEN's apartment.)
(AT RISE: ESTELLE has come to inspect the apartment before GWEN moves in. She unlocks the door, enters, and looks around the room with shock, then with disgust.)

ESTELLE. ... oh, my god. I don't believe this. Pigs ... pigs must have lived here. How can people live like this? *(Goes to the phone, takes phone book out of her purse, dials)* Hello, is this Mary Rose Kessler? This is Estelle Reeves. Estelle Reeves? Gwen's social worker from the group home? We've talked several times? I'm fine, thank you. Mrs. Kessler, we seem to have a problem. I assume you remembered that tomorrow Gwen was being released from the group home? Yes, tomorrow. I called you twice about it and I sent you a letter? And I assume you recall that Gwen was going to share an apartment with another client of mine, a woman named Billie Wills. I believe you spoke on the phone with her once. You don't remember her, either? *(Muttering disgustedly)* Well, it doesn't matter, I guess. At any rate, Mrs. Wills is no longer able to live with Gwen, so of course that makes it impossible for us to carry through with our plans. Our group home has a very long waiting list and Gwen has already been officially released. Her room has been given to someone else. I'm sure there is nothing I could do at this point to get her back into the house. I'm calling you from the apartment your daughter was to have shared with Mrs. Wills. *(Looks around the room)* Mrs. Kessler, it's ... it's ... I'm sure it's not a place where you would want your daughter to live, especially alone. I feel somewhat to blame since I signed the lease without inspecting it first. If I had, I'm sure I would have found it totally unacceptable. The location is ideal since it's close to where Gwen is working and to a bus line, but it's very dirty and quite depressing. Gwen doesn't need that. She needs companionship and a much cheerier atmosphere. Mrs. Kessler ... I guess I'm calling to ask you if Gwen can come home until I can make other arrangements for her. *(Holds the phone away from her ear as GWEN's mother speaks)* Ahuh ... ahuh ... yes, I know your husband is ill. What about Gwen's sister, Kathleen? I know Kathleen already has Gwen's children, but if she could just take her in for a short time, it would give Gwen a ... a safe place to live and it would also allow her to spend some time with her son and daughter. She's only seen them once in the last year, you know. *(Growing increasingly disgusted with the conversation)* I understand, Mrs. Kessler. No, no, I won't call Kathleen. She's already done a lot for Gwen, I agree. Does your daughter have any other friends? Not any? No one she could stay with? Well, let me ask you something, Mrs. Kessler. What do you suggest I do with your daughter? I see. Well, right now I don't seem to have any other choice. Would you come over this weekend and help her get settled in? I'm sure you're very busy and I'm sure your husband is very ill, but your daughter would certainly appreciate the visit. You might want to bring some cleaning things, maybe some sheets and towels. In the meantime, I'll try to find more suitable living quarters for her. Yes, you have a nice day, too. *(Hangs up the phone with anger)* You calloused old bitch. *(Surveys the apartment with contempt again)* There's got to be somewhere else for that girl to live.

(End of scene.)

Scene Two

(SETTING: GWEN's apartment.)
(AT RISE: Enter ESTELLE carrying a bag of groceries. She is followed by GWEN who stands in the doorway holding a suitcase for some time before she actually enters the apartment.)

ESTELLE. The people who lived here before were filthy. I talked to the building superintendent and ... well, for as low as the rent is, Gwen, I'm afraid there aren't too many amenities. He said he'd haul the garbage out, but it looks like we'll have to clean it ourselves.

GWEN. ... it's okay.

ESTELLE. It is <u>not</u> okay. It's ... it's <u>dreadful</u>. But let's look at the good points. Everything has good points, right?

GWEN. ... right.

ESTELLE. It's within walking distance to work. It's small and it'll be easy to clean ... *(Looks around critically)* Once it's clean.

GWEN. ... yeah.

ESTELLE. And the best thing is that it's temporary.

Gwen, I promise that I'll either get you a suitable roommate, or I'll get you out of here. *(Phone rings; GWEN tenses up and stares at it, making no attempt to answer it; ESTELLE is oblivious to the ringing)* Vicky Schroeder's going to be leaving the house soon. She's a very nice person and I know the two of you got along well. She needs a place to live, so -- *(Watches GWEN as she stares at the phone)* Gwen, is there something wrong? Did something happen at work today to upset you?

GWEN. *(Phone stops; she tries to regain her composure)* ... no. Everything's fine, Estelle. It went okay. My supervisor said I did alright.

ESTELLE. Good. How do <u>you</u> think you did?

GWEN. I did ... I did ... fine, I guess. I typed some letters and they mailed them out, so I must have done alright ... I don't know.

ESTELLE. Gwen, just because we won't be seeing each other every day, don't forget our talks. Please remember who the most important person in all of this is.

GWEN. I know ... <u>me</u>.

ESTELLE. That's right. It's you, Gwen. You can't love anybody, not even that little girl and boy, until you love yourself. That's the most important job you have right now. To love Gwen. And then all those other things you told me you wanted so much will happen. They'll just fall into place. *(Phone rings, GWEN tenses up; walks over to it, picks up the receiver and puts it down; ringing stops) (Suspiciously)* What's wrong, Gwen?

GWEN. Nothing. I just wanted ... just wanted to see if the phone works.

ESTELLE. It works. I used it yesterday. I gave the number to your mother and sister. Is that alright?

GWEN. Yeah ... sure.

ESTELLE. There's a meeting at the house next Monday. Don't forget. It's just one bus from here. The 7-A, remember?

GWEN. Yeah, I remember.

ESTELLE. Gwen, you wouldn't be offended if I got some things together to fix this place up, would you?

GWEN. No, Estelle. Of course not.

ESTELLE. *(Walks around the room; a knocking is heard at the front door; GWEN glances nervously from the door to ESTELLE who is oblivious to the sound)* I've got some Cape Cod curtains for that window. I think they're the right length. Let me buy you an apartment warming present. What's your favorite color?

GWEN. *(Thinking)* Uh ... uh ... I guess I don't have one.

ESTELLE. We just painted our living room an ivory color, kind of a soft cream. It's very pleasant, very easy on the eyes. Let me buy a couple more gallons and you and I and maybe your mother and sister can spend an afternoon getting these walls washed and painted. Honey, this place looks too much like a morgue for a girl who's just coming back to life.

GWEN. *(Knocking stops)* ... a morgue?

ESTELLE. That was a poor choice of a word. I'm sorry. We'll get everything in shape and then surprise the kids. They can visit on weekends and if everything continues to go well over time, maybe you can have them overnight.

GWEN. ... maybe.

ESTELLE. So, let's see. You've got your own apartment. *(Looks around critically)* It'll qualify as an apartment soon, at any rate. And you've got a job and you're doing well with it. And we've got a meeting on Monday.

GWEN. Something else, Estelle. At work ... at work ... well, never mind.

ESTELLE. Gwen, tell me. I need to know.

GWEN. Well, it isn't much. It's just that ... I met somebody. Oh, he doesn't know where I live. Don't worry.

ESTELLE. *(Smiling)* He?

GWEN. ... yeah. His name is Jerry. He doesn't work in the office. He works in the factory. Sometimes when I have to take work orders back there, he talks to me. I ... I ...

ESTELLE. You what?

GWEN. I ... ate lunch with him today.

ESTELLE. That's wonderful. So tell me more.

GWEN. *(Phone rings; she stares at it)* ... I told you about all there is.

ESTELLE. There's got to be more than that. What's he look like?

GWEN. *(Trying to ignore the phone)* He ... he's not very good-looking.

ESTELLE. *(Laughs)* So? Either is my husband by most people's standards, and I adore him. Is he nice?

GWEN. *(Shrugs)* ... yeah, he's nice. I don't know him very well, Estelle.

ESTELLE. Give it time. Continue to have lunch with him and talk to him and give him a chance to like you, Gwen. But, honey, this is not, absolutely not the time to get involved with anybody. You know what I mean. Take your time. You'll know when you're in control again and then you'll be able to make the correct decisions involving ... what shall we call it? Your love life? Don't bring him back here, Gwen. And please don't give anyone your phone number. Maybe a girl friend you meet at work, but not a man. Not yet. Promise?

GWEN. ... yes, I promise.

ESTELLE. Besides fixing this place up, you know what else we can do?

GWEN and GWEN

GWEN. What?

ESTELLE. Well, since you have this man interested in you, after the meeting on Monday, I'll arrange for Sherri to cut your hair, okay? *(Touches GWEN's hair)* Let's give you and this place a whole new look. Change, Gwen. That's the key. And all in that easy, comfortable way we talked about.

GWEN. Estelle, do you think <u>everyone</u> can change?

ESTELLE. Everyone who really wants to. Look at yourself.

GWEN. Have you ever tried to help a very ... very ...

ESTELLE. A very <u>what</u>, Gwen?

GWEN. A very ... <u>bad</u> person to change?

ESTELLE. *(Considers the question)* ... I can't think of anyone. Only very <u>sad</u> people, people who were confused for a time. People who were depressed, Gwen. Not bad. There's a big difference between being troubled inside and being bad. Why are you asking me this? Who do you know who's very bad?

GWEN. ... no one.

ESTELLE. Gwen, I don't feel right leaving you alone here. You're acting strangely. I wish I could take you home with me tonight, but I can't.

GWEN. ... I know.

ESTELLE. But I wish I could. If I had my own place, I would. Even though it's against the rules.

GWEN. *(Looks around the room, trying to keep from crying)* This place is just fine, Estelle. Like you said, we'll fix it up. It'll be okay.

ESTELLE. You're not afraid to live by yourself, are you?

GWEN. No, I'm not afraid to live by <u>myself</u>, Estelle. But I can't ... I <u>can't</u> ... live with –

ESTELLE. With who, Gwen?

GWEN. *(Stares at the front door)* With ... with ... my mother.

ESTELLE. Don't worry about her. I don't think you'll be living with her again. By the way, when I spoke with her yesterday, she said she might be coming over to help you clean ... if she can. Your father isn't feeling well, I guess.

GWEN. *(Still staring at the door)* He never does. She has to take care of him.

ESTELLE. Don't make up excuses for her, honey.

GWEN. I'm not, Estelle. My father has always been sickly and she's ... she's a good wife.

ESTELLE. But she's not a very good mother, is she?

GWEN. She's ... she's ... a good wife.

ESTELLE. *(Phone rings; GWEN stares at it and does not listen to ESTELLE)* It's getting late. I've got to get back to the house. Gwen, I'm going to miss you so. I had such hopes for you and Billie. I wanted so much for the two of you to help each other out. I wanted so much for both of you to get your children back into your lives, but Billie's different than you, Gwen. You had a break down and you bounced back, and I really do think you can pick up the pieces and get your kids back, be a family again. But Billie ... well, she's got a different sort of problem. Something much harder to resolve. *(Phone stops ringing)* Speaking of your children, you might want to call them tonight.

GWEN. Not tonight. I'm ... I'm too tired tonight. I want to get the apartment fixed up and then have them over.

ESTELLE. That's fine, but you can call them before that, can't you?

GWEN. *(Getting very nervous)* Not tonight, Estelle. Not tonight.

ESTELLE. Well ... I guess I understand. Listen. I'll call you around nine tonight just to see how you're doing. Then I suggest you go to bed. Don't try and do too much tonight.

GWEN. Estelle, I really do appreciate everything you tried to do for me.

ESTELLE. I know you do. And I appreciate everything you've done for me.

GWEN. *(Confused)* ... I didn't do anything for you.

ESTELLE. You <u>succeeded</u>. You made me feel like I know how to do my job. People make successes of each other, you know.

GWEN. *(Knocking at the door resumes)* ... they do?

ESTELLE. Sure they do. Everyday. I got to go. Talk to you at nine, honey. Love yourself.

(Knocking stops when she exits.)

GWEN. *(Stares after her)* Good-bye, Estelle ... *(GWEN stands in the center of the room for a long time, very nervous and waiting expectantly for something; phone rings; she takes the receiver off the hook, but it continues to ring; she tries futility to ignore it by attempting to make the bed, but becomes increasingly distraught and throws the sheets against the wall; grabs a broom and frantically sweeps the floor; the ringing stops; she stands very still, waiting and listening; a scratching sound at the door begins and slowly escalates into a horrible pounding upon the door; she looks at her watch)* Seven o'clock ... seven o'clock ... Estelle'll call at nine ... at nine. *(Faces the door directly and starts to cry)* I got <u>nothing</u> to say to you! Nothing! I got my own apartment now! You'd just make fun of it, but it's mine! And a job! A job you'd laugh at, but I got a job! And I got a man who likes me, too! *(The pounding continues and the phone begins to ring again)* And I got a friend! Estelle is my friend, and you can say anything about her you want, but she's my friend! You don't have any friends! And I'm gonna get my kids back, too! You can pound on the door and let the phone ring all night, but I got nothing to say to you! I won't talk to you! I won't!

GWEN II. *(The pounding on the door and the phone ringing stop; the door suddenly bursts open; GWEN II is standing in the doorway, looking very annoyed; she is wearing a mink coat and carrying expensive luggage; stares at GWEN, enters the apartment, and slams the door behind her)* What's with you, Gweny? Don't you believe in answering your phone anymore? Your neighbors aren't going to appreciate it if you let your goddam phone ring all the time. They'll report you to the building manager and you'll get your ass thrown out. Besides ... what if it was him? What if he was trying to call you?

GWEN. *(Backs away in fear and shock)* You don't have a key ... how did you open my door? ... only Estelle has a key ... you don't have a key ...

GWEN II. Oh, get off it, Gweny. *(Takes off her coat and tosses it on the bed)* I am the goddam key.

GWEN. *(Weakly)* ... please ... please go away.

GWEN II. Like hell. I need a home just as much as you do. You know what you are, Gwen? You are inconsiderate. You found a home for your kids. You even found somebody to take care of those screwin' goldfish when you moved out. You found a padded cell for yourself to hide in. What about me? What about me, huh?

GWEN and GWEN

GWEN. I was <u>not</u> in a padded cell. I was in a group home and I was free to come and go.

GWEN. II. How nice for you. Well, I <u>wasn't</u> in a home.

GWEN. *(Intrigued)* ... where were you?

GWEN II. What do you care? You got anything to drink? I need a drink bad.

GWEN. No.

GWEN II. *(Goes into her purse and pulls out a bottle of liquor)* I figured you wouldn't, so I had the sense to BYOB it. *(Takes a long drink and critically surveys the room)* What a crummy dump this is. If there's any truth to the theory that people's homes reflect their personalities, you're in big trouble, Gweny. I think she called it a morgue.

GWEN. ... now it is.

GWEN II. A morgue is only for temporary storage. I would prefer to think of this place as a <u>tomb</u>. That implies permanence and that is what we need. Roots. A place to call our own ... forever. Tell your <u>friend</u> she can shove her cape cod curtains and her ivory paint that is so gentle on the eyes. This is fine just the way it is. *(Looks at GWEN for a long time)* You're looking well, Gwen. Certainly better than when we parted company a year ago. *(Pulls out a chair for GWEN)* Come on. Sit down. Have a drink and let's fill each other in on what we've been doing. You know, girl talk.

GWEN. ... please go away.

GWEN II. Only when you do. So how's the kids? They been split up and put into foster homes yet?

GWEN. Get out of here. This is <u>my</u> apartment.

GWEN II. It's <u>my</u> apartment, too. Come on, Gwen. There's enough room for both of us. I don't eat anything. I don't run up utility bills. I <u>can't</u> talk on the phone. I'm the ideal roommate. Sit down. Tell me about this Estelle woman.

GWEN. She's ... she's my friend.

GWEN II. Has she befriended you out of the goodness of her heart, or does she get paid for trying to instill pseudo-confidence in dead-beats like you?

GWEN. She was my social worker at the house. And she's ... she's my friend.

GWEN II. If they took her paycheck away, would she still come around? Would she still be your friend?

GWEN. I ... I think she would.

GWEN II. Let's get her fired and find out.

GWEN. She's going to call me at nine.

GWEN II. So what? Is that supposed to intimidate me? Am I supposed to be scared or something? The Estelle's of the world are a dime a dozen, Gwen. On any street corner you'll find some poor schmuck obsessed with Judeo-Christian ethics. I guess we can let them live, though. They don't do any harm. Don't do any good, either, but they're harmless.

GWEN. ... she's very kind.

GWEN II. Probably kinder than you. Didn't you care what happened to me? Didn't you worry about me for a minute?

GWEN. *(Laughs)* Worry about you? No. No, I never worried about you ... where were you?

GWEN II. *(Ignores the question)* So how's Mom been? Is she still the empathic, selfless incarnation of Mother Earth?

GWEN. My mother is fine and ... my father is not feeling well.

GWEN II. Nobody living with your mother could feel well, Gwen. *(Goes into her purse and takes out make-up and a mirror)* God, I look like shit. What if he calls? What if he wants to come over? I couldn't let him see me like this.

GWEN and GWEN

GWEN. *(In a shaky voice)* He's ... he's not gonna call.

GWEN II. You never know.

GWEN. ... where were you?

GWEN II. So tell me about this job you landed, Gweny.

GWEN. It isn't much of a job.

GWEN II. I'm sure it isn't.

GWEN. I work as an office temporary. I type ... and answer phones.

GWEN II. Sounds fascinating. Did you get it yourself, or did the luny bin get it for you?

GWEN. *(Defensively)* Estelle arranged the interview, but I had to pass a typing and math test by myself.

GWEN II. Congratulations. What did they start you at? Fifty grand?

GWEN. ... minimum wage.

GWEN II. In that case, I suggest you stay out of Sacs. *(Notices GWEN about to touch her mink coat)* Like my coat?

GWEN. *(Pulls away)* What coat?

GWEN II. Good one, Gwen. Estelle really did a number on you, didn't she? I said, do you like my coat?

GWEN. What coat?

GWEN II. *(Throws the coat up into the air and then wraps it around herself)* A man gave it to me. I met him on the plane going to New Orleans. We really hit it off. Spent the next ten days together. It came in the mail about a week after I got home. He keeps calling and writing, but I'm not interested. He was good for ten days in the sack and a mink coat and that's it. Besides, I've got him. Speaking of love lives, how's yours?

GWEN. *(Meekly)* I ... I have a boyfriend.

GWEN II. *(Laughs)* You ate a Granola bar with some fat

slob in a factory cafeteria – once. You call that a boyfriend? I call that nothin'.

GWEN. He's ... he's very nice.

GWEN II. *(Walks up directly behind GWEN and hisses into her ear)* Very nice? By any chance, is that the same thing as fat and boring?

GWEN. *(Pulls away sharply)* Maybe ... but at least he's real.

GWEN II. Pardon?

GWEN. You didn't go to New Orleans and you didn't meet a man.

GWEN II. I can go anywhere I want to, Gwen, and so can you. We used to go all sorts of places together before that bastard fucked us over.

GWEN. *(Frantically)* Don't talk about him!

GWEN II. Sorry.

GWEN. I won't talk about him!

GWEN II. *(Resumes putting on make-up)* So we won't talk about him, lunatic. Shut up and calm down.

GWEN. ... where were you?

GWEN II. So what happened to that broad who was supposed to move in here with you? How come she didn't, huh?

GWEN. Billie ... her name was Billie. She was ... sad. She couldn't take care of her children.

(Reaches out and touches the mink coat.)

GWEN II. Christ, ninety percent of the world is sad. *(Pauses and glances up at GWEN)* Feels nice, huh?

GWEN. *(Pulls away)* Feels like nothin'.

GWEN II. Want to borrow it sometime?

GWEN. Billie ... Billie had to go back to the hospital. She had a relapse, but before that we shared a room in the group home. We talked a lot ... watched television at night. Dr. Jennings saw us twice a week and Estelle spent the days with us. Estelle took us to see some movies and we went to –

GWEN II. *(Cuts her off)* Sounds like a real drag. Two losers who deserted their kids sittin' around watchin' the idiot tube and poppin' antidepressants. I have a feeling I was better off where I was.

GWEN. ... where were you?

GWEN II. We really should celebrate our reunion. Wanna go out?

GWEN. No. I'm going to start cleaning this place and wait for Estelle to call. And then I'm going to bed. I've got to get up early for work tomorrow.

GWEN II. You wouldn't be offended if I didn't accompany you to your place of employment, would you? I can't imagine anything more boring than watching you type memos for eight hours.

GWEN. You haven't changed a bit, have you?

GWEN II. *(Intensely)* Did you expect me to? Did you really think you could put me in permanent cold storage, Gwen? Were you so naive as to think that a few months in a padded cell with some soggy social worker tellin' you that you're really not a fuck-up would get rid of me? *(Approaches Gwen)* It didn't phase me. It didn't alter a single molecule in my structure. All I did was wait ... I just waited.

GWEN. *(Backs away from her)* ... where did you wait?

GWEN II. What the hell do you care? You cared more about those stinkin' gold fish than me! You actually called somebody the day before you moved into the nut house and asked them if they would be so kind as to look after your kids' stinkin' fish!

GWEN. *(Laughs)* Were you envious? Envious of two gold fish?

GWEN II. *(In a dire and serious voice)* I'm <u>envious</u> of every lousy thing in this world, Gwen. You know that. And don't laugh at me, or I'll slap that smile off your ugly face. Don't laugh at me and don't abandon me again.

GWEN. Why won't you tell me where you were?

GWEN II. Because you want to know. If you didn't want to know, I'd force it down your throat. *(Phone rings; GWEN II turns and stares at it)* Answer it. It might be important. It might be somebody sellin' storm windows. It might be a lucrative job offer. It might be Rebecca of Sunnybrook farm callin' to tell you to love yourself.

GWEN. ... no.

(Phone stops.)

GWEN II. Why didn't you answer it?

GWEN. Because you wanted me to.

GWEN II. *(Laughs)* Touche, Gweny. Oh well, now we'll have to wonder for the rest of our lives who it was. Anybody come to visit you at the nut house?

GWEN. It wasn't a nut house. It was a group home.

GWEN II. Six a' one, half dozen a' the other. Anybody come to visit you?

GWEN. Kathleen ... and the kids came once.

GWEN II. What about Mother Earth? Did she come?

GWEN. You think you're so smart ... so smart. Did she come?

GWEN II. That Estelle did a good job on you.

GWEN. You're actually giving somebody a compliment?

GWEN II. Oh, I wouldn't go so far as to say that, Gwen. No, I think she's a phony and she only helped you because the state paid her to do it, but she did do her job. However, don't develop any delusions.

GWEN. Delusions about what?

GWEN II. About the battle between good and evil, between Estelle and me. There's no competition there. I could crush her skull if I wanted to. I could mutilate her with my magic words. I am the sorceress, not her. I am the key. I have the magic. And I can prove to her just what a miserable failure she is.

GWEN. You are so jealous ... so jealous ... where were you?

GWEN II. *(Turns away from GWEN and seems to withdraw into herself)* I ... I ... was ... on the dark side of the moon.

GWEN. *(Very curious; approaches her)* Where is that? What does that mean?

GWEN II. I ... I ... was in a terrible place. At least you had people of sorts to talk to and drugs to pacify you and potholders to make. I had <u>nothing</u>.

GWEN. There were no people there?

GWEN II. People? *(Turns to glare at GWEN)* <u>People</u>?! There was <u>nothing</u>. Not a single life form. It was a dark place ... it was night all the time. There were no ceilings or floors or walls and yet ... yet ... I was not free. Not free at all. I was just suspended there, like a puppet on strings that seemed to go up, but didn't attach to anything.

GWEN. Where was it?

GWEN II. Sometimes I thought I heard voices. Well, not really voices. <u>Howlings</u>. I heard howlings ... like animals that wanted to die, but couldn't. And I had lost my voice. I tried to howl, too, but nothing came out ... nothing. No sounds came from me. I voicelessly screamed for you, Gwen. I screamed and moaned and wailed in silence. I swung back and forth on those strings until they were in knots. I tried to untangle them, but I couldn't, so I tried to bite through them, but they weren't made out of something you can bite through. I struggled and cried and cursed you, Gwen ... I cursed you in silence, Gwen.

GWEN. ... but how did you get free?

GWEN II. You freed me, Gwen.

GWEN. *(Astonished)* ... I didn't free you.

GWEN II. Sure you did. After a time that felt like eternity, I began to feel you tugging at me. The strings loosened and fell away. The evil puppet was free and the darkness started to get a little bit brighter. I could hear your voice. It was soft at first, but I waited. I bided my time since time was all I had, and sure enough. Your voice became louder and louder. Then I felt you tugging at me. I saw a path. I also saw my mink. I put it on and started walking. Pretty soon you were pulling at me so hard that I could barely keep up. I had to run and I stumbled, but you kept tugging. And then one day ... I don't know ... maybe yesterday, maybe last night, I just found myself in the hallway outside this dump. I kept calling and calling so as not to be rude and just walk in on you, but you wouldn't answer your fucking phone, so eventually I just let myself in.

GWEN. ... I didn't free you.

GWEN II. You still don't understand, do you, Gweny? Did you ever have an I.Q. test when you were a kid? What'd you score? Forty, fifty maybe? You freed me. *(Starts to back GWEN up against the wall)* You liberated me, Gwen, and I am very grateful. And just to show you my gratitude, I as well as Estelle have an apartment warming present for you. *(Hits GWEN across the face and causes her to fall on the bed)* There! And don't you ever <u>dare</u> send me away again! Don't you ever <u>dare</u> lock me in that prison without time and light and sensation and purpose! Don't you dare deny <u>me</u>! Don't you ever again pay some jailor to suppress me into nothingness so you can pretend for a few months that you're sane! Now go to bed, Gwen. Get your beauty sleep. You need it. You look like shit. *(Puts on the mink)* I'm going out for the evening. If <u>he</u> calls, just take a message.

(Exits, slamming the door.)

GWEN. *(Runs frantically to lock the door after her; phone rings)* Hello? Oh, Estelle, it's you ... it's you. No, I'm alright, honest. Thanks for worrying, but I'm alright. *(GWEN II returns and stands behind GWEN; recites the remainder of the conversation along with her)* Well, I've been cleaning up. Sweeping, and I made the bed. No, I haven't eaten yet, but I will. Don't worry about me, Estelle. The kids? Maybe I'll call them tomorrow after work. No, I haven't forgotten the meeting on Monday. I'll be there. Thanks, Estelle ... good night. *(Hangs up, glares at GWEN II)* I didn't set you free!

GWEN II. *(Shuts the door)* If you didn't, Gwen, then who did? Who freed me? Mother Earth? Estelle? The shrink with the pill pad? The gold fish?

GWEN. I don't know, but it wasn't me. Now go away. Go out for the evening, as if you had anyplace to go.

(Drops down on the bed.)

GWEN II. *(Contemplates GWEN)* You look so forlorn, so victimized sitting there. I just don't have the heart to go out and have a good time when you're suffering so, Gweny. Would you like me to stay in tonight and comfort you?

GWEN. <u>You</u>? Comfort <u>me</u>? That'll be the day.

GWEN II. *(Sits down on the bed next to GWEN)* Did I tell you the fish died, Gwen?

GWEN. Huh?

GWEN II. The fish. The goldfish you found the good home for, dimwit. They died. Mrs. ... whatever her name was flushed 'em. Actually, she forgot to feed them, so they starved to death.

GWEN. Who cares?

GWEN II. I thought for sure you would. After all, you took great pains to find them a home. I figured they must have meant something to you ... more than I meant to you.

GWEN. *(Shakes her head in disbelief)* I don't believe it. You're actually jealous of two fish ... two <u>dead</u> fish.

GWEN II. Believe it, Gwen. Believe it. It's like I told you before. I am a master of envy, and her sister, jealousy. But I can't take all the credit for that accomplishment myself. I had truly <u>marvelous</u> instructors. *(Sits down at the table and resumes fixing her hair and make-up)* Yes, Gwen, I am envious of everything in this lousy, stinking world. I'm envious of everyone whose parents are kind and wise and rich and who grew up smart and pretty and loved. I'm envious of every human being who was ever happy. I'm jealous of every woman _he_ touched, every woman he wanted, every woman who laid down with him. And yes, Gwen, I'm jealous that you cared more about those smelly fish than me ... _me_ ... your only real friend.

GWEN. It's funny the way things turn out, isn't it? I wanted the fish to be taken care of, I wanted them to live ... and I wanted you to die.

GWEN II. That's life. When have you ever really gotten what you wanted, Gwen?

GWEN. I'm very tired ... have to get up at six-thirty and go to work.

GWEN II. So go to bed then. You don't mind if I watch TV for awhile, do you?

GWEN. I don't have a TV set.

GWEN II. *(Points to the refrigerator)* That looks like a TV set to me. With cable and movie channels no less. I'll watch a movie and you go to sleep.

GWEN. It's not a TV set ... it's a refrigerator. And I don't care what you do with yourself.

(Lies down and covers herself.)

GWEN II. *(Walks over to the bed)* Want me to tell you a bedtime story, Gweny?

GWEN. No.

GWEN II. Oh, come on. You just take a few deep breaths and relax and I'll lull you to sleep with a story, just like Mommy never did. *(Sits on the edge of the bed)* Do you want a fairy tale? A Harlequin romance? A famous classic? I know a lot of stories.

GWEN. ... I'm not listening to you.
GWEN II. How about a <u>horror</u> story?
GWEN. I said I'm not listening.
GWEN II. How about a <u>true</u> story? Those are always the most horrible, you know. The most incredible imagination in the world couldn't begin to make up the horror that really exists. You want to hear one? I got a <u>good</u> one. Once upon a time there was this house. It wasn't like an ordinary house with a mommy and a daddy and a VCR and a cat and two fish and a couple of crummy kids with snotty noses and a microwave on the sink. This house was full of crazy people. Oh, no one called them crazy. That would have been rude. They called them <u>sad</u> and depressed and temporarily socially incapacitated, but they were all crazy. They couldn't function like normal people, whatever the hell <u>normal</u> people are. And ... a particular room in this crazy house was shared by two women. They were both sad ... very sad. And every night their fairy godmother would come into their room and tell them to love themselves because they really were wonderful people deep inside. Well, one of those two sad women, the older one ... I think her name was <u>Millie</u>, she figured that if other people could love her, then she could love herself. So she decided to see if she could get her sad, sad roommate whose name was <u>Gwenevere</u> to love her. One night after the fairy godmother had gone home to her very normal family and very normal house in an affluent upper middle class suburb where she could forget about the leper colony where she did her good deeds, Millie jumped into bed with Gwenevere and asked her point blank if they could be lovers. Now, Gwenevere was crazy, but she was also heterosexual, when she could get it which wasn't often. So she told Millie

<u>no</u>, also in a point blank fashion. Welllll, <u>poor</u> Millie who so wanted to be loved so that she could love herself just couldn't cope with the rejection. So she slit her wrists and got sent back to the <u>real</u> <u>big</u> nuthouse where she underwent painful electric shock treatments and a frontal lobotomy. If Gwenevere had been a little more charitable and a little less sexually conventional, maybe Millie would have gone home, feeling loved, and gotten her children back. But as it turned out, Millie got a straight jacket and a fried brain and her children got given to the state. And only Gwenevere got to go home. The end. *(Tucks the blanket around GWEN)* Now go to sleep, honey.

GWEN. *(Throws the blanket off and sits up)* You don't know what you're talking about!

GWEN II. *(Goes back to the table where she continues to fix her hair)* Don't I?

GWEN. You didn't know Billie! She had a lot of serious problems and that wasn't the first time she tried to kill herself!

GWEN II. Then why do you feel so guilty? Why do you feel responsible? Why do you worry about her kids so much?

GWEN. *(Jumps out of bed)* I don't feel responsible! I just feel ... sorry. I feel sorry for her. She was my friend ... and I met her children. They were nice little kids.

GWEN II. Are your kids nice little kids?

GWEN. Yes, the nicest kids in the world. And I'm going to get them back just as soon as I can. I can worry about other people! I can feel sorry for other people! That doesn't mean that I feel responsible for their problems.

GWEN II. Why didn't you ever tell Estelle about that little incident, huh, <u>Gwenevere</u>? You sure as hell told her everything else.

GWEN. What was the point in telling Estelle? Billie had a lot of problems and Estelle knew what they were.

GWEN II. You knew why she tried to kill herself, but you never opened your big mouth about it. You feel guilty, Gwen. It's as simple as that.

GWEN. I do not feel guilty! I do not feel responsible!

GWEN II. Gwen, honey, you are the guilt. And I am the jealousy. You were always the one who felt certain that every time somebody got shit on, it was your fault. It was something you did. You got convinced a long time ago that everything was your fault and, like the fool you are, you believed it. You were the one who took the blame and I was the one who hated. You were the martyr and I was avenger. What a pair, what a team.

GWEN. *(Goes into her purse and frantically searches around; pulls out three dollars and shoves then into GWEN II's hand)* Here! It's all I got! Take it! Take it and get out! Go out and have a good time! Just get out of here!

GWEN II. *(Contemplates the money and then GWEN)* With three dollars? I can't spend money. You know that. We've been apart for so long that you've forgotten the rules. *(Balls up the money and tosses each dollar at GWEN as she states each rule)* First, I can't answer the phone. Second, I can't spend money. And third, I can't go until you go.

GWEN. ... but you can let me sleep.

GWEN II. That I can do.

GWEN. I'm tired ... I have to go to work in the morning.

(Exits into the bathroom and puts on her nightgown.)

GWEN II. *(Fondles her mink coat)* This is going to be a real challenge. This place is a hole, a hole in the ground. Oh, well ... it's better than nothing. It's ... it's a home again. I need a home just as much as you do! I'm just as human as you are! You may not think so, but I am. I'm certainly more human than those goddam fish!

GWEN. *(Comes out of the bathroom)* You still talkin' about those fish? Look, console yourself with the fact that they're dead.

GWEN II. Oh, I do find consolation in that fact. As a matter of fact, if they weren't dead, I'd go over there and kill the little shits myself.

GWEN. You gonna kill my kids, too, because I found them a home?

GWEN II. No. You're doing that yourself very nicely in a more round about and socially acceptable way.

GWEN. *(Stares at her and slowly gets into bed)* ... I love my children and I will get them back.

GWEN II. I see. Well, good luck, Gwen. At any rate, it will take me awhile to forgive you for leaving me out in the cold.

GWEN. It'll take forever. You never forgive anybody for anything. You hold on to everything ... everything you should throw away.

GWEN II. That's correct. That's one of my primary tasks. As a matter of fact, it's in my job description. To remember, to recall, to recollect, and to alphabetically file the vermin of life away. To preserve it systematically so that it can be retrieved at a moment's notice.

GWEN. What about the good things? What about the happy times? Do you have a file for those, too?

GWEN II. What good things? What happy times?

GWEN. Nobody's life can be completely devoid of happiness ... can it?

GWEN II. That depends on how you define happiness, Gwen. Your definition of happiness came along only once ... and he dumped your ass.

GWEN. I said I wasn't going to talk about him. Don't get me upset anymore tonight. *(Lays down and pulls the blanket over herself)* Watch a movie on the refrigerator if you want, but shut up and let me sleep.

GWEN II. It's a deal, but let's say our prayers together first.

(Goes to the foot of the bed and kneels.)

GWEN. Don't ... please.

GWEN II. Gwen, we need some religion back in our lives. *(Folds her hands in prayer)* Dear ... whoever ... great spirit ... please bless Gwen and her nicest kids in the world ... and her caring mother and sickly father ... bless her lesbian friend in the state asylum for the hopelessly insane and your handmaiden, Estelle, who does your work here on earth.

GWEN. Stop it.

GWEN II. *(Grabs GWEN's hands and forces them together in prayer between her own)* Don't interrupt me while I'm in prayer, heathen. Bless the fat and boring man with whom she breaks bread in the factory and let her memos be without typographical errors ... and lastly, welcome her beloved gold fish into everlasting life. Amen. *(Pushes GWEN down on the bed; goes to the refrigerator and pretends to turn a button on)* Oh, Gwen, Casablanca's on! What luck!

END OF ACT

ACT II

(SETTING: GWEN's apartment one week later. Nothing has been cleaned up or put away and the room looks noticeably worse than before. GWEN looks more haggard and GWEN II looks more beautiful and elegant than in Act I.)

(AT RISE: GWEN II is alone on stage. She reaches into a box near the table, pulling out GWEN's photo album; as she opens it, a child's drawing of flowers falls out; she appears to be mesmerized by the picture; gingerly picks it up, holds it up to the light and stares at it; GWEN's key in the door brings her back to reality; sits down and appears to be paging leisurely through the album as GWEN enters.)

GWEN II. Good evening, Gwen. Type any interesting memos today?

GWEN. *(Enter; takes her coat off)* ... did anyone call?

GWEN II. Nope. *(Looks at GWEN)* What?! No stunning new hair style? I thought Sherri was supposed to turn you into a homecoming queen after the meeting.

GWEN. I didn't go to the meeting.

GWEN II. Why not?

GWEN. *(Shrugs)* ... I don't know.

GWEN II. Because you didn't want to listen to Estelle's you are somebody dribble. You are a child of the universe with a right to be here. However, you hoped the phone would ring. You hoped Estelle would come looking for her little pseudo somebody. Well, sorry, Gweny. No phone calls.

GWEN. You think you know everything, don't you?

GWEN II. *(Returns to looking at the album)* Hardly. I just happen to know everything about you, Gwen.

GWEN. You know, all day at work I had this wonderful dream, this fantasy that I would come back to this god-awful place and find it empty. Maybe a few rats and bugs running around, but I wouldn't mind that. I kept picturing myself opening the door and finding ... nothing. Maybe just a note from you on the table. Dear Gwen, I've gone back to oblivion. Good-bye.

GWEN II. Dream on, Gweny. Dream on. People need their dreams. That's what keeps them going. Remember our dreams before he came long? We had some pretty good ones, didn't we? Remember all the places we were gonna go and all the money we were gonna spend? He really knocked the hell out of our dreams ... but not mine. I'm still enjoying myself. Know where I went today?

GWEN. *(Sits down wearily on the bed)* Please don't tell me ... when are you gonna leave?

GWEN II. Only when you do.

GWEN. ... why?

GWEN II. I don't know. Maybe we should take some psychology courses and find out. *(Walks over to the bed and shows GWEN the album)* Aren't these islands beautiful? That's where I went today.

GWEN. That's a picture of my sister in front of my old house.

GWEN II. Not necessarily. It could be Greece. *(Walks around the room and flips through the album)* Funny thing,

GWEN and GWEN

Gwen. There aren't any pictures of you as a kid in here. How come?

GWEN. I don't know.

GWEN II. There's Kathleen, and there's your brothers, but none of you. How come the old lady never took any pictures of you?

GWEN. I already told you. I <u>don't</u> know. My parents were poor, I guess. They couldn't afford stuff like that.

GWEN II. But they could afford to take pictures of Kathleen?!

GWEN. Look! Let's drop the subject. I'm not interested.

GWEN II. Then ... then why do you think about it so much?

GWEN. *(Stands up and stares at GWEN II)* Why ... why do <u>I</u> think about it? <u>You're</u> the one who thinks about it. I didn't bring it up.

GWEN II. *(Closes the album and puts it next to the phone)* Do you think she didn't take any pictures of you because in order to look through a camera and photograph something, you must have at least <u>some</u> awareness of its existence?

GWEN. *(Furious)* Don't start on me the minute I walk through the door! I'm tired!

GWEN II. Forgive me. Why don't you sit down and relax and let me tell you about my trip to Greece? I met the most <u>fantastic</u> man there!

GWEN. No! Because you didn't go to Greece! You've never been out of the state in your miserable life!

GWEN II. <u>He</u> went to Greece. Remember him telling us that? I wonder if <u>he</u> ever took <u>her</u> there.

GWEN. Stop it!! I just finished my first full week of work! It was very difficult for me! Now leave me alone!

GWEN II. You call that work?

GWEN. Yes, I call that work. I don't mean typing and answering phones. I mean being with people again, having to communicate with people ... with normal people. Having to act like ... like ...

GWEN II. Like a normal person?

GWEN. ... yeah.

GWEN II. When you look at it that way, I guess it must have been pretty rough on you, Gweny. How did you ever do it?

GWEN. I did it because you didn't come with me. I suppose I should thank you for that.

GWEN II. You should. Did you eat lunch with Jerry again?

GWEN. ... you know I did.

GWEN II. How exciting.

GWEN. He asked me for my phone number.

GWEN II. Well, whoopee shit! How could you give it to him, Gwen? How could you sink so low after him?

GWEN. ... Jerry is nice.

GWEN II. Nice and fat.

GWEN. Jerry is also real.

GWEN II. Yeah, real fat.

GWEN. No! I mean real real. Not like your men ... not like ... him.

GWEN II. Then I guess I prefer insubstantial beauty to flesh and blood horror.

(Tenses up and looks around the room, sniffing.)

GWEN. What's the matter with you?

GWEN and GWEN

GWEN II. I smell a rat! Someone's coming. There's a strong odor, a powerful stench. It's ... it's a woman, I think. She has a firm, fast step. She means business. It's ... it's Medea!

GWEN. *(Frightened)* ... Medea?

GWEN II. Better known to you as Mother Earth.

GWEN. *(Panicky)* My mother!? My mother!? I don't want to see her! I don't want to talk to her!

GWEN II. I don't blame you, Gwen. Maybe you're sane after all.

GWEN. What should I do?! Are you sure it's her?! It's not Estelle?!

GWEN II. Estelle and your mother have distinctly different odors. Estelle is stale and flat, like day old bread. Mother Earth is pungent and severe. Almost gamy like two day old garbage sitting in the sun. Sorry, Gweny. I know your mother when I smell 'er.

GWEN. *(There is a firm knock on the door)* You go away! You go in the bathroom! Don't talk to me!

GWEN II. That's fine with me. You're not exactly asking me to make a sacrifice.

(Goes into the bathroom and leaves the door partially open.)

GWEN. *(Trying to get control of herself)* Who's ... who's there?

MOTHER. It's Mom, Gwen.

GWEN. *(Leans her head against the door)* Mom ... Mom ... you didn't call ... I wasn't expecting you.

MOTHER. *(Enters and looks critically around the room)* Good lord ... your social worker didn't knock herself out looking for an apartment for you.

GWEN. ... it's okay, Mom.

GWEN II. *(Sticks her head out of the bathroom door)* It's a diseased hovel!

MOTHER. I know the rent's cheap, but really Gwen. There must be rats and roaches here. *(Goes out into the hall and comes back with a box of cleaning items)* Have you heard any rats? Seen any bugs when you turn the lights on?

GWEN. Um ... a few.

MOTHER. *(Approaches the bathroom; GWEN II stands in the doorway, smoking a cigarette; GWEN rushes to stand in front of her)* Is that the bathroom?

GWEN. Yes.

MOTHER. God only knows what's in there.

GWEN II. God and you, Mom. Don't you recognize me? I'm that contraceptive failure from thirty-three years ago.

MOTHER. I'm ... I'm shocked that Ester would put you in a place like this.

GWEN. Estelle, Mom. Her name is Estelle.

MOTHER. Whatever. She could have found you a nicer place.

GWEN II. *(Comes out of the bathroom)* Unbeknownst to herself, Ester found your daughter the perfect place, Mother. It suits her well.

MOTHER. *(GWEN gestures for GWEN II to go back and her mother looks at her curiously)* Gwen ... what's wrong with you?

GWEN. ... nothing. I'm alright, Mom.

MOTHER. I assume they released you because you're well now.

GWEN II. You always viewed the world through such simplistic eyes, woman. She's not well at all. She's incurable. That's why they released her, but she won't tell you that.

GWEN. ... I'm doing a lot better, Mom.

GWEN II. See? What did I tell you? Tell her you're crazy, Gwen! For God's sake, tell her you're mad!

GWEN. *(Trying to ignore GWEN II)* ... I'm ... I'm doing much better.

MOTHER. No matter where we lived, Gwen, no matter what kind of place we lived in, I always kept it clean. You've been here for over a week. Don't tell me you haven't had time to clean. Surely you have nothing else to do in the evening.

GWEN. Mom ... it's been hard for me. Hard to go back to work. I guess when I come home, I feel ... I feel ...

MOTHER. *(Impatiently)* You feel like what?

GWEN II. Like not cleaning, you moron.

GWEN. I feel ... sort of ... depressed.

MOTHER. *(Takes a rag and cleaner out of the box and starts cleaning the sink)* Everybody gets depressed, Gwen. Do you think you're the only person in the world who gets depressed? Besides, I thought that year you spent in that ... that ...

GWEN II. Nut house.

MOTHER. That ... home was supposed to make you well again. I don't have the heart to tell your sister what your apartment looks like or what you're acting like after she took your children in for an entire year and almost ruined her marriage over it.

GWEN. ... ruined her marriage?

GWEN II. Don't fall for that one, Gweny. Your sister's been divorced twice and she's lived with three men. She couldn't have a decent relationship with a man if her life depended on it. But, if you insist, go ahead and feel responsible. That's part of your job description.

MOTHER. Well ... I didn't want to tell you before. I tried to keep a lot of things from you for awhile, but Ralph and Kathleen are not getting along. They have three children of their own and your two only complicate matters for them.

GWEN II. Don't fall for it, Gweny. If they had no kids or fifty kids, they'd still beat each other up. Your sister's a bitch and Ralph's a drunk who hits women. But go ahead. Wallow in guilt. You do it so well.

GWEN. Kathleen never said anything, Mom. I didn't know.

MOTHER. She wanted to spare you.

GWEN II. Kathleen didn't tell you because she never thought for a minute that your two little darlings were ruining her marriage. It's a trap, Gwen. *(Comes up behind GWEN and hisses into her ear)* Don't fall in.

MOTHER. I took the children on several weekends to take the pressure off your sister, but your father just couldn't take it. He's sick, Gwen. You know that. His nerves can't take two children yelling and picking on each other.

GWEN II. Not to mention your nerves, Mom. Every time she doesn't want something, she says your father doesn't want it, Gwen. Your old man is a shriveled-up, hen-pecked wimp who never wanted or didn't want anything in his life. He's got no opinions. He's got no desires. He's a vegetable, Gweny! He never even noticed when you kids were in the house!

GWEN. *(Moves away from GWEN II)* I ... I know I've been a big inconvenience to everyone, Mom.

GWEN II. Oh, Christ. The martyr is emerging. Do you mind if I go into the bathroom and puke? *(Turns, starts to go into the bathroom, then turns around in anger)* You weren't a big inconvenience, you worm! Your sister and your old man are so screwed up they didn't even notice your kids!

MOTHER. We all cared about you and we all tried to help you, Gwen. Why don't you do something? *(Hands GWEN a rag)* Start wiping out those drawers. There's probably rat droppings in there.

GWEN II. *(GWEN II begins to follow the MOTHER around stage, dropping cigarette ashes on whatever surface she has just finished cleaning)* So what if we happen to like rat droppings? They're part of the tomb decor. Where there's corpses, there's rodents.

GWEN. *(Fearfully opens a drawer and starts to wipe it out)* I never expected Kathleen to take care of the kids forever.

MOTHER. Well, I should hope not. You had them, Gwen. You married a man I begged you not to marry and had children with him. I warned you he'd never support you. You wouldn't listen, and now those children are your responsibility. Not your sister's and certainly not mine.

GWEN II. There are no surprises with this woman. She is a constant in the universe, a predictable and steadfast force not unlike the forces of physics. She is incapable of change, Gwen, so don't expect it from her. She can't change anymore than you can.

GWEN. *(Turns to GWEN II)* I can change!

MOTHER. ... I hope so, Gwen. I hope this year has not been a complete waste for you and your family. Men have affairs and leave their wives all the time, every day. Life has to go on after that. I have never been able to understand why you allowed yourself to fall to pieces like you did.

GWEN. Mom ... Mom ... I guess ... it was more than that.

GWEN II. Not only do you view the world through simplistic eyes, woman, but you have a mind to match. A simple-mindedness that is a phenomenon in its own right. If you had raised a human being, his jilting her would have caused merely a temporary despondency, short-lived and of no consequence to the remainder of her life. But you instead raised a ... a <u>subhuman</u> thing, a missing link, homo sapien in appearance, but sadly lacking the knowledge that it was indeed human. His jilting her caused her to crumble because she did not possess that one vital trait of the soul that separates humanity from the beasts.

GWEN. *(Stares at GWEN II)* ... and what's that? What's that?!

MOTHER. What's what?

GWEN. *(Flustered)* Nothing ... nothing ... I thought I heard something.

(Starts to cry.)

MOTHER. *(Stops cleaning and looks critically and unsympathetically at GWEN)* Snap out of it, Gwen. I came here because I promised your social worker I would help you clean this place up. I did <u>not</u> come here to listen to you whine.

GWEN. I'm sorry. I've just ... just got a lot of problems, Mom.

MOTHER. Well, don't blame them on me. I did my best, Gwen.

GWEN II. You did your best to fuck up your kids.

MOTHER. You can't go through life blaming other people for your problems, Gwen. At some point in time you have to take the responsibility upon yourself and shape up – *(GWEN II speaks with her)* Or ship out!

GWEN and GWEN

GWEN. You're right ... you're right. *(Regains control of herself and stops crying)* I'm grateful for everything you've done for me.

GWEN II. Oh, Christ! Grateful for what? What'd she ever do for you?!

MOTHER. *(Starts to sweep the floor)* Your father and I did our best, Gwen. We didn't have much to work with, but we did our best for the four of you. We always had food on the table.

GWEN. ... yeah.

GWEN II. I've never been one to quote scripture, but someone did say something like "children do not live on mashed potatoes alone." So you gave her enough food to keep her alive so you wouldn't be arrested for child neglect. Big fucking deal! What about her!? What about her?! *(Points angrily to GWEN)* No wonder she got locked up. No wonder she can't get a decent job. No wonder she can't raise her kids. She can't do a goddam thing except ... eat mashed potatoes.

MOTHER. You've had your year of relaxation. Now it's time to get back to work.

GWEN. *(Astonished)* ... I wasn't relaxing, Mom.

MOTHER. Well ... whatever you were doing. Anyway, it's over now and you need to take your children off your sister's hands.

GWEN II. Fine. Send them right over. They can move in with the rats and the roaches and she can support them on welfare wages and they can all starve together. And Kathleen and Ralph and you and Daddy can all live happily ever after. I mean, what are families for?

GWEN. *(Confused; glances between GWEN II and MOTHER several times)* Mom ... Mom ... what is it you want me to do? Exactly what do you want me to do?

MOTHER. I want you to stop thinking about yourself, Gwen. Think of your children. They are far more important than you.

GWEN II. Estelle just got done telling her that <u>she's</u> the most important person in the world and <u>not</u> her kids. You're confusing this poor animal, Mom. Who's she supposed to believe?

MOTHER. You were always a self-centered girl who looked for attention, Gwen.

GWEN II. <u>Any</u> child who is chronically ignored by its parents looks for attention, you dimwit!

MOTHER. I think you've had enough attention for one year, don't you?

GWEN II. You never once came to visit her in the nut house, lady! Are you gonna come to her funeral, huh? Are you gonna bother to show up when she's buried?

MOTHER. Your Aunt Delores calls me and asks me how you are and I never know what to say to her because I never knew what was wrong with you in the first place.

GWEN II. Well, at least you embarrass her, Gwen. At least you elicit <u>that</u> much of a response.

MOTHER. Your sister's divorced and she's been jilted by men, but <u>she</u> didn't abandon <u>her</u> children.

GWEN. Mom ... I guess you just don't understand.

MOTHER. I understand that you better get your life back together and soon. Real soon, Gwen. Now, I've come to help you. Let's get some work done around here.

GWEN II. *(GWEN and MOTHER clean and do not speak)* You always did have a peculiar way of helping people, Mom. You know what I'll always remember about the way you help people, Mom? The day her husband walked out on

GWEN and GWEN

her. He left her with two little kids and not a pot to piss in. And you were right, I'll give you that much. He was a bum. She married him against the only good advice you ever gave her. And she was frantic when he left, so who did she run to? Who else? Mother Earth. That proverbial safe harbor in the storm of life. If I remember correctly, and I always do, you took sides with the son of a bitch you'd been condemning since day one. You said she was a lousy wife. *(GWEN stops cleaning and stares at her MOTHER)* She told you that he hit her, and you, Mother, said that she probably deserved to be hit. She probably <u>asked</u> for it and then you proceeded to order her out of your house. Yes, Mom, you always did have a peculiar way of helping people. The next time Aunt Delores calls and inquires as to the condition of Gwen Kessler, just tell her that Gwen died. That will make it easier for you.

GWEN. *(Turns and stares at GWEN II)* Mom ... you better go home. Dad ... Dad might need you. I can finish this.

MOTHER. But will you?

GWEN. Yeah ... sure. I'll clean this weekend. Thank you for coming over.

MOTHER. I was always clean, Gwen, and I didn't raise my children to live in pig pens.

GWEN II. Yeah, yeah, yeah. You were always clean and there was always food on the table. You want a <u>medal</u>, bitch?

MOTHER. *(Puts on her coat and prepares to leave)* And I want you to tell that ... that ... Evelyn –

GWEN. Estelle?

MOTHER. Yes, Estelle. That Estelle woman that I <u>did</u> come over. I always get the feeling from her that she thinks I don't care about you.

GWEN II. Astute woman, that Evelyn.

GWEN. I'll tell her you were here, Mom. *(MOTHER starts to exit)* ... Mom?

MOTHER. What, Gwen?

GWEN. I meant what I said before. I'm grateful for everything you've done for me.

MOTHER. *(Smiles coldly at her)* I'm sure you are, Gwen. In your own way, I'm sure you are.

(Exit)

GWEN II. Get outta here, you bitch!! *(Picks a can off the floor and hurls it at the door)* When are you gonna give the hell up?! Just because there's some obscure, unwritten code of human ethics that says you're supposed to feel gratitude towards your parents, you don't necessarily have to go along with it! Name <u>one</u> thing she ever did for you! <u>One</u> stinking thing! And <u>don't</u> say – *(In a wimpy voice)* ... she gave me my life.

GWEN. She never did anything for me. I just feel sorry for her.

GWEN II. The martyr again. You're really into this martyrdom stuff, aren't you? Go ahead and feel sorry for her. God knows, I can't stop you. But I <u>hate</u> her. I hate her filthy guts. You know, I could never figure out why people like her have kids in the first place. And they always have so goddam <u>many</u> of them. It's weird. Clearly they don't want them. They don't love them. They possess the parenting skills of a fucking rattlesnake. People like her aughta be sterilized. They shouldn't be allowed to breed.

GWEN. She could never be anything. She never went any place. She never learned anything. My father never gave her anything. You've got to feel sorry for someone like that.

GWEN and GWEN

GWEN II. Like hell you do.

GWEN. *(Laughs)* You sound like Estelle.

GWEN II. Whoops! I better watch what I say. Let's change the subject, alright?

GWEN. Let's don't change the subject. You know, you don't have to remind me of all those things ... all those ... those terrible things.

GWEN II. Yes, I do. That's my job. Remember? To file away the vermin of life, to preserve it. If I don't do it, who will?

GWEN. Why does anybody have to do it?

GWEN II. Now you sound like Estelle. I don't know the answer to your question, Gwen. I don't know why somebody has to do it. You know, when I was in the netherworld, when I was suspended there in the great silence that was only occasionally broken by the howls of animals, I tried to speak.

GWEN. Yes, you told me. And nothing came out. It's hard to imagine nothing coming out of your mouth.

GWEN II. My mind was filled with thoughts and ideas and observations and revelations, and my mouth and tongue and lips and teeth went through all the necessary contortions. I had the will, the desire to speak, to communicate with you, with anybody who would listen to me ... but no sound came forth. *(Comes up behind GWEN)* Is that how you feel sometimes, Gwen? Is that how you feel when that old bag attacks you? Is that how you felt when you called his apartment and that woman answered? Were you just bubbling over with verbalizations, but mute? Quiet? Afraid?

GWEN. I'm not like you ... I can't talk like you.

GWEN II. Is that why you didn't tell Estelle why your roommate tried to kill herself?

GWEN. I'm not like you.

GWEN II. Is that why you didn't order that lying bitch out of your apartment a few minutes ago?

GWEN. I said I'm not like you!

(Phone rings.)

GWEN II. *(Turns abruptly towards the phone and stares at it)* Answer it!

GWEN. No! You answer it! You're the one with the big mouth! With the voice! With the communication skills!

GWEN II. But I'm not the one with the power, dummy! Answer it!

GWEN. *(Picks up the phone)* Hello? ... hello? *(Hangs up)* They hung up.

GWEN II. Too bad. It might have been him. Maybe he wanted to get back together with you.

GWEN. And you have the audacity to call my mother cruel? My mother is kind. She is thoughtful and caring compared to you.

GWEN II. You mother is a diseased woman who spread her sickness to her children. She is not kind.

GWEN. And don't talk to me about him! Don't talk about him! It took me a whole year to come to terms with losing him! I'm not going to let you destroy the progress I made.

GWEN II. Progress? Look around you, Gweny. Look at this mess. Does this look like the home of a woman who's made progress?

GWEN. *(Looks around and then closes her eyes)* ... yes. Because all it means is that I'm out of the group home. It doesn't matter what the place looks like. What matters is that I'm out of there and on my own.

GWEN II. Where are your kids? You haven't got the guts to call them. You call that progress? You still can't stand up to your mother. You call <u>that</u> progress? You make four bucks an hour and you live with rats and bugs. You call <u>that</u> progress?

GWEN. I told you ... the place doesn't matter. Nothing matters. I made progress. I got out of the group home.

GWEN II. And what did you move into? A place that makes the group home look like a goddam sorority house at Vassar. Estelle knew what she was doin' when she moved you into this place. She knew you'd fit right in.

GWEN. Estelle rented this apartment because it was cheap and close to the office where I work and she didn't have a chance to see it before she signed the lease.

GWEN II. Do you believe that?

GWEN. ... why shouldn't I?

GWEN II. Do you believe you love your mother?

GWEN. ... why shouldn't I?

GWEN II. Do you believe you're ever gonna clean this place up?

GWEN. *(Starts to cry)* ... maybe I will.

GWEN II. Do you believe you're ever gonna see those sweet little kids again?

GWEN. *(Grabs her coat)* I believe I'm getting outta here. I'm going to the house, to the meeting.

GWEN II. I know. Well, I hope you have a nice time.

GWEN. *(Turns and looks suspiciously at GWEN II)* ... you promise you won't come with me?

GWEN II. I promise.

GWEN. *(Starts to exit and then stops)* ... why?
GWEN II. *(Shrugs)* I get tired, too, you know.
GWEN. No, I guess I didn't know that.
GWEN II. Oh, not tired like you. Not a physical tiredness. It's a different kind of fatigue. I get tired of you, Gwen. I get tired of what a spineless, uninteresting loser you are.
GWEN. Do you promise?
GWEN II. Good-bye, Gwen. Give my best to Estelle. *(GWEN exits; GWEN II contemplates the phone for a long time)* Damn her. Damn her to hell. *(Goes to the phone and picks up the receiver)* Let's see ... Mother Earth ... Kessler ... Kessler. Come on ... you can do it.

(Very clumsily dials the number; the sound of the phone ringing can be heard and then MOTHER's voice.)

MOTHER. Hello? Hello? Who's there? Who's there?
GWEN II. *(Contorts her mouth and face and tries to speak, but no sound comes out; slams the phone down)* Shit! Fuck! *(Pages through the phone book)* Estelle ... what the fuck is her last name? Reeves ... Estelle Reeves.

(Clumsily dials the number and the same thing happens.)

ESTELLE. You have reached the residence of Dr. Robert and Estelle Reeves. So sorry no one is home right now, but you and your message are important to us. At the sound of the tone please leave your name and message and the time of your call and we'll get back to you just as soon as we can. Bye now and have a very nice day.

GWEN II. *(Waits for the tone and then tries to speak; no sound comes out; slams the receiver down and then knocks the phone off the table with great rage; as the phone falls, the photo album lying by the phone falls also; she sees the flower drawing lying on the floor; stares at it and then gingerly picks it up)* Are ... are your kids nice little kids? Yes ... yes, the <u>nicest</u> little kids in the world ... and I'm going to get them back just as soon as I can ... just as soon as I can ... just as soon –

(Lets the drawing drop to the floor, grabs her coat and exits.)

END OF ACT

ACT III

(SETTING: It has been a month since GWEN moved into the apartment and no attempts have been made to clean it up. It is filthier than before. GWEN II is more stunning and glamorous than before and GWEN looks worse than ever. She is pale, has dark circles under her eyes, malnourished and very poorly dressed.)
(AT RISE: GWEN enters, looks around the apartment and then at a newspaper clipping lying on the floor.)

GWEN II. *(From the bathroom)* That you, Gweny?
GWEN. ... who else? Who else?

(Picks up the clipping and reads it.)

GWEN II. *(Enters brushing her hair; she is wearing an evening gown and is heavily made up)* I'm in kind of a hurry. Got a date tonight. *(Looks over GWEN's shoulder)* Where'd you get that?
GWEN. *(Puts clipping into GWEN II's hand)* Right where you put it.
GWEN II. She is attractive for an old broad. Kind of dried-up, but well-preserved, like a mummy. What do you think?

(Shows clipping to GWEN.)

GWEN. *(Pushes it away)* I've seen it. Why did you save it?

GWEN II. I didn't save it. You saved it. Says here she works for an accounting firm. You finish high school, Gweny?

GWEN. You know I did.

GWEN II. They went to the Dominican Republic on their honeymoon. Must have been with her money, huh? That lazy son of a bitch had trouble gettin' outta bed to go down to the unemployment office. *(Contemplates the picture)* The Dominican Republic, huh? Sounds nice. And after they return the happy couple will reside in ... paradise. Huh! They'll reside in paradise if I let 'em.

GWEN. ... what's that supposed to mean?

GWEN II. *(Crumbles up clipping and throws it in the sink)* It means I might decide to go over there and burn their goddam house down, that's what it means.

GWEN. *(Takes the paper out of the sink and unfolds it gently)* ... yeah, she is attractive. What in God's name did he ever see in me?

GWEN II. He saw me in you. He saw this gorgeous creature. We were one then, Gwen.

GWEN. ... oh, no. I was never you ... I was never you.

GWEN II. Sure you were, you dumb shit. You sure you finished high school? You're awfully stupid, Gwen. *(Phone rings)* Answer it. I'm expecting a phone call.

GWEN. *(Sits down wearily at the table)* No, you're not.

GWEN II. Answer it!

GWEN. Who'd call you?

(Phone stops ringing.)

GWEN II. <u>Him</u>! *(Points to the clipping)* He was supposed to call tonight.

GWEN. ... he's married.

GWEN II. So what? That doesn't mean I can't see him anymore. Maybe he wants to have an affair with me. Maybe that old broad ain't so great after all.

GWEN. ... you're crazy.

GWEN II. Pardon me? <u>Who's</u> crazy?

GWEN. You are.

GWEN II. Let's try that again. <u>Who's</u> crazy?

GWEN. Leave me alone. When are you gonna leave?

GWEN II. Just as soon as I change.

GWEN. No, I mean when are you gonna leave and never come back ... never?

GWEN II. Oh, <u>that</u> when am I gonna leave. You don't want me to go. Think about it. What would happen if I left you for good? What the hell would happen? Come on.

GWEN. ... I'd be ... I'd be free.

GWEN II. Hey, I ain't your prison. I ain't your jailor. Your poverty is. Your stupidity and cowardice. <u>They're</u> your prison. Not <u>me</u>. Can't you see two inches in front of your nose? I'm your <u>freedom</u>, you little fool. Look at me. *(Spins around in a circle)* You can be and have anything you want through me, Gwen. I am the key! I am the sorceress! I have the magic! I can fly out of this prison any time I want! I can sprout wings! I can become things! The bars of the cell can't contain <u>me</u>! My essence passes between them like mist! *(Looks at GWEN with a sudden sense of astonishment)* You haven't forgotten that part of me ... have you?

GWEN. *(Rubs her forehead)* Go out on your stupid date. I've got to call my sister. I've <u>got</u> to ... I've been here for a whole month and I've only talked to her twice.

GWEN II. *(Rubs her own forehead in the same fashion)* Don't give me your headaches. Don't inflict your guilt on me.

GWEN. What guilt?

GWEN II. The guilt that is obviously consuming every morsel of your being at this moment and causing you to develop a migraine tension headache. And you can pop aspirins till you puke blood, Gwen, and nothin's gonna get rid of that pain. Go ahead. Call your sister. Think up another flimsy excuse why you can't see your kids.

GWEN. I want to see them ... I do ...

GWEN II. Sure, sure you do.

GWEN. *(Runs her hands over her face and chest)* I look so bad. I don't want them to see me like this. And this place. It's ... it's ...

GWEN II. It's a pig sty.

GWEN. I don't want them here.

GWEN II. You're rationalizing and you know it. And you're not even doing it well. I know why you don't want to see those kids and you know why you don't want to see those kids, so why play games?

GWEN. You're so smart ... so smart. You think you know everything.

GWEN II. Not everything, Gwen. I don't know jack shit about nuclear physics or organic chemistry or the Civil War, but I do know about you.

GWEN. Then tell me. Why don't I want to see my kids?

GWEN II. *(Hesitates)* ... I don't think you can handle it right now. You'll get upset and we'll start arguing again and I'll be late for my date.

GWEN. You don't have a date! Tell me!

GWEN II. No, I will not tell you. And you're wrong. I do

have a date. Remember ... I can have anything and anybody I want. I'm not the one locked in prison.

GWEN. He's married. He's been gone for over a year.

GWEN II. Hey, those minor details don't make any difference in this neck a' the woods. Go call your sister. Make up another lame excuse for neglecting your kids, and then come out with us.

GWEN. You and him?

GWEN II. If you come along, it'll be us and him ... just like old times.

GWEN. *(Weakly)* ... he's married.

GWEN II. Only if you say so.

GWEN. *(Sits by the phone and dials her sister's number; GWEN II is sitting at the table, putting on her make-up)* Hello? Kathleen, it's me ... Gwen. I'm okay. How are you? My job? Well, it's only good for three more days and then ... I don't know. I guess the agency will find me another place to work.

GWEN II. Somehow I doubt that.

GWEN. ... how ... how are the kids? *(Starts to shake and cry)* Kathleen, can you give me a little more time? My apartment still needs a lot of work ...

GWEN II. *(Kicks the garbage out from under the table)* That is an understatement.

GWEN. And ... and I don't feel very good. I really do miss the kids, though. Who? Oh, ... Jerry. Well, yeah, I still see him at work. We went out last Saturday. Yeah, it was alright.

GWEN II. *(Disgusted)* It was an enormous waste of time!

GWEN. We went to a bar near where we work and had a drink ... nothing special.

GWEN II. Nothing special is right. You would have had a better time if you stayed home and scrubbed out the toilet.

GWEN. ... he's ... he's nice.

GWEN II. He's a bore. A big, fat stupid bore.

GWEN. ... yeah ... I guess I like him.

GWEN II. Liar! He makes you sick!

GWEN. Estelle? No, I haven't heard from her in a while.

GWEN II. That's because when you moved out of the nut house, Estelle no longer got paid by the state to coddle you. Some friend, huh, Gweny? Some friend.

GWEN. Kathleen .. how are things between you and Ralph? He did? He left?

GWEN II. Big deal. So what else is new under the sun?

GWEN. I'm really sorry, Kathleen. I hope you can patch things up with him. I'll try real hard to get over this weekend. No, you don't have to pick me up. *(Looks frantically around the room)* No, please don't! I can take the bus. Thanks, Kathleen. I owe you about a million favors by now.

GWEN II. The only favor she wants from you is to get your crummy kids out of her house. That will suffice nicely.

GWEN. *(Frightened; stiffens up)* What? Talk ... talk to the kids? *(GWEN II becomes frightened also; stands up and stares at GWEN)* Um ... I want to ... I really do ... but maybe I shouldn't right now. *(GWEN II appears relieved and sits down again)* I will soon ... soon. Tell them I said hello. Tell them ... tell them that I love them.

(Hangs up.)

GWEN II. How touching. Remember what Estelle said. You can't love anybody till you love yourself. Do you love yourself, Gwen?

GWEN and GWEN

GWEN. I hate you.

GWEN II. I guess that answers my question.

GWEN. I hate you and I'm trying to love myself.

GWEN II. You got shit for brains, Gwen. You still don't get it, do you? You're stupid and you're also a pathological liar.

GWEN. Oh?

GWEN II. You had a lousy time on that so called date with Jerry. You were miserable. He tried to hold your anemic little hand and you almost puked. You wanted so badly to be with him, and there you were with fat, boring Jerry. The walking, breathing incarnation of mediocrity.

GWEN. Jerry's –

GWEN II. *(Cuts her off)* I know, I know. Jerry's nice. Do you have any idea how many times you've said that? Christ, Gwen, the dog who lives in the building superintendent's apartment is nice, too. As a matter of fact, you pat that little doggy on the head every night when you come home from work and you don't get nauseated when you touch it, but Jerry's touch made you want to barf. I guess that dog is nicer than Jerry, huh?

GWEN. Shut up.

GWEN II. Come on, Gweny. Come on. Do yourself a favor for once in your life. Come on the date. It'll be us and him. Nice and cozy. We'll go to that little bar. Remember the little bar downtown with the blue candles on the tables? We'll go sit way back in a corner and he'll fondle our legs under the table. And we'll drink Chablis and chit chat about what's going on in our lives, our plans, our travels, our next book, our stock portfolio. And we'll pretend that our parents were kind and educated and that we went to graduate school and we've been to Paris. And then we'll leave, holding hands, and we'll go back to his place and screw our brains out till the cows come home. Sounds like fun, huh? Sounds better than sittin' around here, waitin' for Jerry to call and ask you in his monotone, semi-mentally retarded voice if you want to meet him for a beer in some stinking bar by a factory.

GWEN. ... why do you say those things to me?

GWEN II. What things?

GWEN. Those things about ... about Jerry ... about my children. Why do you talk like that?

GWEN II. I beg your pardon. I don't talk like that. You talk like that. I don't hear me. I hear you. If somebody walked in here right now, who would they see? Just you, sittin' around talkin' to yourself. Seething, sulking, being eaten away by various and sundry neuroses. *(Points to GWEN's head)* I don't know if you know it or not, but you ain't got much left up there. You're becoming dysfunctional. I don't think the office temporaries are gonna give you another job, and that's pretty bad, Gwen, 'cause those suckers'll hire anybody.

GWEN. *(Angrily)* Alright! Alright! And why am I crazy?! Huh?! Why am I dysfunctional? Does it have anything to do with you? With your existence?

GWEN II. It has to do with you, with your existence.

GWEN. ... then where do you come in?

GWEN II. I come in whenever you let me in. I come in when you're vulnerable, Gwen. When you're alone, when you walk through that door. I come in when you hate yourself and when your guilt is eating you up like a cancer. I come in when it's dark and you can't sleep. Gwen ... Gwen ... I'm all that's left of your dreams, so treat me with kid gloves. You know what happens to people who lose their dreams, don't you?

GWEN. You said it yourself. They seethe and sulk and eat themselves away.

GWEN II. That's just the beginning. The final stages of the disease are worse than that. My advice to you at this despondent moment in your life is to come with me. I'm the only one who can help you. You think that stupid shrink at the group home with his head up his Freudian ass helped you? Hell, no! You think Mother Earth is gonna help you? Think again, sweety. You think that crummy traitor Estelle can help you? God, she cut you off like a dead branch as soon as she stopped getting paid to bail you out. What the hell ever happened to that ivory paint that is so <u>easy</u> on the eyes? *(Hits the wall with her fist)* Do you see it, huh? I don't see it! These walls still look like shit to me! And those Cape Cod curtains never did get hung, did they? <u>Did they</u>?!

GWEN. ... I guess not.

GWEN II. You're damn right they didn't. Come with me, Gwen. *(Stretches out her hand)* I can take you anywhere. Far away from this miserable life. I am the key. I am the sorceress. I have the magic ... you haven't forgotten that part of me, have you?

GWEN. *(Backs away from her)* ... he's gone ... he's married.

GWEN II. Did you ever read your chart in the nut house?

GWEN. No, they didn't let us ... why?

GWEN II. Well, I did. Want to know what that head shrink wrote down about you? He said you were neurotic bordering on psychotic. He called you a manic depressive and one of the worst masochists he's ever seen. He described you as a latent lesbian with a serious personality disorder due to critically low feelings of self-worth who was potentially homicidal.

GWEN. You're lying! You're making that up!
GWEN II. Like hell I am.
GWEN. He didn't call me those things! He called you those things!
GWEN II. Okay. He called us those things! All except one. That he did mean exclusively for me.
GWEN. What ... what was that?
GWEN II. Potentially homicidal.
GWEN. *(Frightened)* What's that supposed to mean?
GWEN II. It means that son of a bitch who dumped us and got married to Miss Mummy Face with her CPA and her Volvo is finally, finally going to care about us when I point a gun in his stinking face.
GWEN. *(Terrified)* No ... I couldn't kill anybody ... not anybody.
GWEN II. You can if I help you.
GWEN. No ... no ... you get away from me.
GWEN II. Gladly. I give up, Gwen. I've got to put the finishing touches on for my big date.
GWEN. I want you to tell me why I don't want to see my kids.
GWEN II. Sorry, I haven't got the time right now. Look, I'd love to stay and chat. I just adore our conversations, but I've got a man waiting for me. This is your last chance to come along.
GWEN. *(Sits down on the bed)* ... you don't have anybody or anything waiting for you.
GWEN II. *(Goes to the door and pretends to let someone in; then goes back to the table and sits down)* Hi, Sweetheart. It's so good to see you. I just hate it when you have to leave town, but I love it when you come back. So, how was the west

GWEN and GWEN

coast? I'm glad you were bored. I'd hate to think of you having a good time without me. Well, I certainly haven't been bored. Been working too hard. God, I love my job! *(Turns to see if GWEN is watching)* I work with the most super people. I wouldn't mind staying there for the rest of my life. I probably will, too, considering the promotions they've promised. Oh, guess what? I finally got my car. <u>Finally</u>! It's so beautiful. Walk me out back later and I'll show it to you. I'll let you drive it around the block for a kiss. *(Kisses the air; phone rings)* Well, answer it, dumbbell! And why are you staring at me? You've heard all this before. Hey, go wash the dishes or kill a cockroach or something. You didn't want to come along, so butt the hell out. This is a private party. Oh, I'd love to go. Friday night is fine. Answer the phone, goddamit!

GWEN. *(Phone stops ringing)* ... no.

GWEN II. Let me see ... where was I? Oh, I'd love to go. Friday night will be fine. <u>I don't have any children</u>, so I'm footloose and fancy free.

GWEN. *(Stands up)* I have two children ... two children ... a boy and a girl.

GWEN II. That's right. Over there, you have two children. Over here, there aren't any children. The woman in the picture ... <u>she</u> didn't have any kids.

GWEN. I have a feeling you're trying to tell me something, and I don't think I want to hear it.

GWEN II. Too late. You've already heard it. You've known it all along, anyway. You don't want to see your kids, Gwen, because you <u>hate</u> your kids. You convinced yourself that he dumped you because of the kids. He was never a <u>family</u> man. You knew that. You got yourself knocked up twice, thinking that would make him stay with you, but it didn't. He was a selfish, lazy bastard who didn't want no responsibilities. He wanted a woman to support him and no kids in the picture. And when he found what he wanted, he dumped your ass.

GWEN. *(With increasing rage)* ... get out ... get out of my house! Get out of my house!

GWEN II. Remember that night you called him and <u>she</u> answered, as if you could forget? What did he tell you, Gweny? He was living with some rich old broad who didn't have any kids, was not interested or available, and hung up on you. Remember what you did that night?

GWEN. ... I ... I cried myself to sleep.

GWEN II. Remember what you did <u>before</u> you cried yourself to sleep?

GWEN. ... I don't remember.

GWEN II. Sure you do, you liar. You slapped the girl across the face, told her it was <u>all</u> her fault that he left you, and you didn't feed either one of 'em for <u>three</u> days. The girl went to school, bruised and wearing dirty clothes. The boy sat in a corner and cried while you laid in bed in a drunken stupor, pissing and moaning over the fact that that stupid asshole left you. The school called the county child abuse authorities and next stop, Estelle's nut house!

GWEN. <u>Get out</u>!

GWEN II. Oh, the truth is an ugly thing, isn't it? That kid had a welt that covered her face. The cops took a picture of it.

GWEN. <u>Get out</u>!

GWEN II. It's not that simple, Gwen. If only it were. You're weird, you know. You <u>demand</u> that I tell you something and when I finally comply, you scream at me and order me out of the house. Why?

GWEN. I do not hate my children!

GWEN II. You got a few bucks. Certainly enough for busfare. Get on a bus and go see 'em. Give 'em a big hug and a kiss. Bring 'em back here. Live with 'em. Pull yourself out of the swamp, Gwen. Go ahead.

GWEN. *(Turns away and buries her face in her hands)* I'm too ... too ashamed. I can't yet. I can't, but I will. I swear I will.

GWEN II. Do you mind if I get back to my fantasizing now after I was so rudely interrupted?

GWEN. It was ... it was ... fantasy?

GWEN II. That's not the issue, honey. The issue is what do you need to keep you going? When we were one person, we had dreams. We had fantasies that kept us alive and well. But you can't dream anymore, Gwen. You forgot how to do it ... and now you're dying.

GWEN. He's gone ... that's what's real and that's what I have to accept. Dr. Jennings said that's what I have to accept. He said I needed to replace him in my life.

GWEN II. With Jerry? How are you gonna meet men? You look like shit. Here. Look at yourself. *(Grabs her make-up mirror off the table and tries to force GWEN to look in it)* Look at yourself! You got no money to go out or to buy clothes with. You got no car. You got no self-esteem and every hang-up on earth. You're probably frigid and you got nothing to say to anybody. *(Contemplates GWEN)* I know the truth hurts, but cheer up. Aw, come on, honey. Let's try and be like we were before that bastard came along. We had some pretty good times then. We were ... fused.

GWEN. ... fused?

GWEN II. Yeah. We were really one person then. We shared the same deams, remember?

GWEN. ... what dreams?

GWEN II. <u>What</u> <u>dreams</u>? Oh, Christ, Gwen, we had <u>dozens</u> of dreams! I know! Let's play a game. Let's play fantasies. You come and sit down. *(Leads GWEN to the table and forces her into a chair)* Sit down! I'll act out one of our favorite fantasies and you see if you can remember it. *(Looks around the room)* I need a prop for this one. *(Goes into the refrigerator and takes out a bottle of ketchup; clutches it to her chest and clears her throat)* You ready? I would like to thank my mother who sacrificed and denied herself so much over the years to pay for my acting lessons, my devoted and supportive husband, my <u>marvelous</u> director, and the members of the academy for giving this to me! *(Holds up the bottle and then kisses it; looks at GWEN)* Remember that one? That was one of our all-time favorites. *(Forces the bottle into GWEN's hands)* We won the Oscar!!

GWEN. *(Pushes the bottle away and stands up abruptly)* This is ridiculous! That is a bottle of ketchup. We're alone in a filthy, god-forsaken apartment, and I've got eight dollars to my name.

GWEN II. You're a real drag, you know that? *(Phone rings)* Obviously someone is trying to reach you. You may as well answer it. It might be your sister. Maybe one of those kids you love so much got hit by a car.

GWEN. Why did you say that!?

GWEN II. On the other hand, it might be Triple-A wantin' to sell you a membership.

GWEN. Why are you so intimidated by the phone?

GWEN II. ... I'm not intimidated by <u>anything</u>.

GWEN. No matter how deep into never-never land you are, you always notice the phone. How come?

GWEN and GWEN

GWEN II. Answer it, Gwen. It might be Jerry, wantin' to buy you a beer. *(Phone stops)* And of course ... it might have been ... him.

GWEN. ... I'm going to bed.

GWEN II. It's five-thirty in the afternoon, you ninny. Keep me company, Gwen. *(Grabs GWEN's arm and pulls her back to the table)* I'm here alone all day. The highlight of my day is when you walk through that door. Sit down. Let's play some more fantasies. Maybe that will make you feel better. *(GWEN lethargically allows herself to be seated)* I know you're real upset about hating your kids and all, but it's okay. Really. Lots of people hate their kids. Look at your mother.

GWEN. ... I do not hate my –

GWEN II. *(Cuts her off)* Now, another one of our favorite fantasies was the wedding.

GWEN. Wedding? ... what wedding?

GWEN II. Our wedding to The Most Wonderful Man In The World. Remember him? We never gave him an official name. Just The Most Wonderful Man In The World. Surely you haven't forgotten him, Gwen!? Remember all his classy friends and the violins and champagne and us floating in a cloud of taffeta and lace and joy beneath the rose trellises? Don't worry about your family members embarrassing you. I had the good sense not to invite them.

GWEN. I'm not interested in this wedding.

GWEN II. Of course you are! It's your wedding, you dope! Come on. Let's march down the aisle. *(Grabs GWEN, but she pulls away; GWEN II proceeds to march across the room, singing to the tune of Here Comes the Bride)* Gwen is a slut. Can't sell her butt. Got dumped so often that now she's a nut.

GWEN. Shut up!

GWEN II. Here's another one. Gwen is a whore. Jerry's a bore. He's so disgusting she won't let him score.

GWEN. *(Jumps up and screams)* Stop it!

(Throws herself on bed.)

GWEN II. *(Contemplates her)* Get hold of yourself, Gweny. It's only a dream ... it's only a fantasy.

GWEN. ... I don't want to fantasize with you.

GWEN II. Fine, but then we need to think of something else to do for entertainment this evening. Um ... I know! Let's tell each other secrets.

GWEN. I don't have any secrets. You know everything about me.

GWEN II. True. But ... um ... I've got a few secrets. A few little tidbits I've kept from you.

GWEN. Then keep them to yourself now. I'm tired ... I want to go to sleep.

GWEN II. I've never been very good at keeping secrets, Gwen. They're just oozing out of me. *(Goes to the bed and reaches in between the mattress; pulls out a handgun wrapped in a rag)* Secret number one. *(Waves it in GWEN's face)* Remember this?

GWEN. *(Jumps off the bed and backs away in fear)* ... no.

GWEN II. Oh, come on, Gweny. Sure you do. Last month? Meeting at the nut house? Sneak upstairs afterwards, hoping that crazy Billie, the mad lesbian, forgot to take her gun from beneath the floorboards. *(Uncovers the gun and waves it over her head)* Well, she forgot!

GWEN and GWEN

GWEN. I didn't do that! <u>You</u> did!

GWEN II. You still don't get it, do you? It doesn't matter, though. It's not important <u>who</u> took it. The secret has to do with <u>why</u> someone took it. It seems to me the thief convinced herself that she lived in a bad neighborhood and needed protection.

GWEN. That's right. That's exactly why.

GWEN II. Nope. Big, fat rationalization. The secret is that she wanted to protect herself from <u>herself</u> when things got too ugly. It's got two bullets. How symbolic. One for you and one for ... <u>me</u> ... the <u>bad</u> neighborhood. Two little pieces of metal, aimed at the right vital organ in the right direction and you won't have to think about <u>him</u> anymore. You won't have to think about your mother or those wonderful, wonderful kids who you starved and beat or Jerry's fat arm around your shoulder.

GWEN. No! All I want is to be rid of <u>you</u>! If I thought bullets would kill you and let me survive, I'd empty a machine gun into your head!

GWEN II. Such violent talk from such a wimp. *(Holds the gun out to GWEN)* If it will make you feel any better, you can empty these two into my head. It might be therapeutic for you, might release some of the tension ... but ... but they'll pass through me like concern for your children passes right through you. I'm as indestructible as your fears. I'm as impervious as your weakness.

GWEN. Everybody's got an Achilles heel. I just haven't found yours yet.

GWEN II. That's another secret I've kept from you. You've always had the power to destroy me, just like Dorothy always had the power to return to Kansas, but she was too involved in the whole mess to figure it out. When you're covered up to your eyebrows in shit, it's pretty hard to see, or breathe, or move. If you could just wipe some of the shit away, maybe you could regain a little of your ability to reason. But you, Gweny, are a romantic. And romantics love to wallow in shit.

GWEN. *(Knocks the gun out of her hand to the floor)* Jerry said he's gonna call me! And I'm gonna go out with him! And I'm gonna call my kids! You wait and see!

GWEN II. You're just on a high, Gweny. You'll come down. You always do.

GWEN. Maybe, but I'm gonna call my kids. I might even clean this place up.

GWEN II. No, you won't ... you can't.

GWEN. *(Frantically)* Yes, I can! And I can get a roommate! I can find someone to live here with me! I need people around. People! Real people. I can put up a notice at work or run an ad in the paper. If I had someone else around, it would crowd you out!

GWEN II. *(Laughs)* Who the hell would move into this dump with you? Not even Jerry if you offered him your ass ten times a day. I mean, really, Gwen. Would you pay rent to live in a rat-infested hovel with a masochistic, depressed, homicidal neurotic who talks to herself all night and keeps a loaded gun laying around? I'm the only roommate you'll ever get.

GWEN. I'm not trapped! I'm not!

GWEN II. Yes, you are. You're like a caged animal in the fucking zoo and very few visitors bother to stop and look at you. You're not interesting enough and I scare them off.

GWEN. ... there's got to be some way to get out of here.

GWEN and GWEN

GWEN II. Only with tremendous effort, and you don't have the cognitive or spiritual strength to accomplish it. At least, not tonight. Let's have a party! A <u>dinner</u> party. *(Looks through the cupboard)* I'll fix us a nice dinner. Let's see ... we got half a box of Bisquick with roaches in it, some stale wheat thins that the rats have been nibbling on, a jar of moldy jelly and some stadium mustard. Christ, Gwen, no wonder we're starving. *(Slams the door shut)* Looks like we'll have to skip the entrees tonight. How about booze and cancer sticks?

(Goes into her bag and pulls out a bottle of scotch.)

GWEN. ... where did you get that bottle?
GWEN II. Look familiar?
GWEN. Yeah. Where did you get it?
GWEN II. I found it lying on the path back from oblivion. It's the very same scotch you were drinking when you beat up that daughter you love so much. *(Pulls out a chair for GWEN; she sits down and GWEN II pours liquor into two glasses)* Drink up. Bon appetit.

GWEN. *(Takes the glass)* ... why don't I trust you?

GWEN II. Why the hell should you? I don't even trust me. Let's drink a toast.

GWEN. Let's not. Let's just drink. *(Gulps down the drink)* God, this stuff is horrible! I hate hard liquor.

GWEN II. Sissy. I guess it was you all along who couldn't hold our booze.

(Fills GWEN's glass, but does not drink her own.)

GWEN. I'm getting sick to my stomach. I haven't had anything to eat in days. I think I better lie down.

(Stands up unsteadily.)

GWEN II. *(Grabs her arm and prevents her from leaving)* Party pooper! Don't leave me here to drink alone. You know what they say about people who drink alone. Have one more. It'll help you sleep. Maybe you'll get through a whole night without waking up every hour and thinking about what a marvelous life you've had. That would be nice. Admit it.

GWEN. *(Accepts another drink)* I always envied depressed people who coped with their depression by sleeping.

GWEN II. An enviable trait indeed. There's nothing worse than misery and insomnia to keep you wallowing in it all night. But then ... I don't speak from experience. I don't sleep. How's about another secret?

GWEN. *(Pours herself another drink)* How's about not?

GWEN II. Secrets aren't any fun unless you blab them. Secret number three. I'm your insomnia, Gweny. It's been me all along who wakes you up in the dead of night. I sit on the edge of the bed and watch you sleep just long enough to keep you alive, and then I sort of ... *(Pushes GWEN)* Nudge you around a little. You've always been a light sleeper. You wake up and then we start over.

GWEN. *(Growing increasingly drunk and nauseated)* Why ... why?

(Phone rings.)

GWEN II. *(Tenses up)* Answer it!
GWEN. *(Starts to go to the phone and then stops)* No ... you're not waking me up tonight.

GWEN II. Answer it! It might be Jerry, Gwen! My god, it might be Jerry!

(Phone stops ringing.)

GWEN. *(Pours the remainder of the bottle in her glass)* You're not waking me up tonight.
GWEN II. I know ... I know.
GWEN. I hate you. Did I ever tell you that?
GWEN II. In wine there is truth. In scotch there is even more truth. Especially scotch in the anemic, malnourished bloodstream of a guilt-ridden neurotic.
GWEN. You bet it's the truth! I'll become an alcoholic if it will keep you from waking me up at night.
GWEN II. Oh, you won't have to go that far, Gwen.
GWEN. *(Speech is slurred)* But ... but I will.
GWEN II. What!? And give your mother and Estelle who care so much about you additional reason for worry? Don't you think it would be slightly illogical for you to purposely become drunk right now with all your other problems?
GWEN. Not if ... not if ... it'll keep you away from me.
GWEN II. Well, then why stop there? Hell, start on drugs, too. Pills. Tranquilizers and antidepressants and crack and heroin. You can become a prostitute to buy them. Now, think of this, Gwen. Then you'll be a neurotic masochistic manic depressive homicidal lesbian drug addict alcoholic call girl! You'll have cornered the market of fuckupaphobia! You'll be an infamous case in the police files, not to mention the psychology journals. Maybe Psychology Today will ask you to do a centerfold.
GWEN. I haven't really slept since you came back ... you know that? One night ... just let me sleep for one night.

GWEN II. I'll let you do more than that. *(Backs over to the gun, picks it up and holds it behind her back)* Gwen ... how much do you hate me?

GWEN. A lot.

GWEN II. Do you love me ... at all?

GWEN. No.

GWEN II. Then we'll have to do it out of hatred rather than mercy. I had hoped it could be different. I'm not all bad. I prefer mercy over hatred, but you just set the rules.

GWEN. ... rules for what?

GWEN II. For our grand finale.

GWEN. What are you talking about?

GWEN II. This. *(Holds the gun out)* This is a strange situation we're in, you and me. You can't pull the trigger on me because it won't kill me. And I can't pull the trigger on you because I don't have the power. So ... you know what that means. You'll have to do it to yourself.

GWEN. *(Jumps up clumsily and knocks her chair over)* I won't! Put that thing down! I'm going to sleep and tomorrow Jerry's gonna call! He said he would! And I'm gonna clean this place! I'm gonna wash these walls and I'm gonna get my hair cut! And I'm gonna call my kids! I'm gonna get on the bus and I'm gonna go to Kathleen's and get my kids!

GWEN II. Oh, please! Don't make me laugh, Gwen. Our predicament is far too morbid for jokes. And your pathetic little plans for the future have no power over me. I've grown too strong, Gwen. I am the fortress. I am the prison. I am the cage. You are trapped, my dear. And trapped animals chew their legs off. Here. *(Forces the gun into GWEN's hands)* Chew your leg off.

GWEN. *(Starts to cry)* ... I'm ... I'm afraid ... of you.

GWEN II. Of course you are, honey. I am the nightmare. Of course you are. *(Grabs GWEN's hands and tries to get her to aim the gun at her head)* Do it! Get it over with!

GWEN. *(Struggling)* No!

GWEN II. You're a loser, Gwen. A loser. You know as well as I do that pumpkins don't turn into golden carriages and frogs ain't fucking princes. He's gone. He's married ... and he ain't <u>ever</u> gonna call you again.

GWEN. But ... but you used to say ... you used to say he might call!

GWEN II. Don't be an idiot, Gwen. He hasn't called in years!

GWEN. No! You say he'll call!

GWEN II. Don't you see how ridiculous, how pathological all of this is? He's <u>married</u>. Do it, Gwen. Put a dignified end to this ... this <u>joke</u> ... this <u>farce</u> we've become.

GWEN. *(Staring at the gun)* ... no ... no.

GWEN II. I know how things turn out for people like you. I can see your past and I can see how you got to where you are tonight. And worst of all, I can see where you're headed, and it ain't to no comfortable life in the upper middle class with a goddam new car and a trip to <u>Jamaica</u> every winter. All I see for you ... for us ... is an extension of this madness and ... and death.

GWEN. *(Still contemplating the gun; in a very weak voice)* ... things can change ... people can make things change.

GWEN II. What kind of people? <u>Your</u> kind?

GWEN. ... any kind ...

GWEN II. <u>My</u> kind?

GWEN. ... any kind ...

GWEN II. *(Laughs)* <u>Our</u> kind? No! We're the means for comparison that other people need in order to see how good they've got it. Gwen ... I know I've put you through hell, but now I want to help you.

GWEN. ... no, you don't know how to help anybody.

GWEN II. I certainly do! Look! The moment that we became severed was the moment that this was guaranteed. The writing was on the wall. I saw it. Why didn't you? You're supposed to be the <u>realist</u> in this relationship. Do you think any person has ever survived this kind of amputation?

GWEN. ... we ... we can reunite.

GWEN II. No. It's futile. It's like trying to repair severed nerves. You can't do it. It takes a powerful chop to cut a person in two like this, but when it happens, there's no point in going on.

GWEN. *(Staring at gun; growing increasingly mesmerized by it and weaker vocally)* ... he came along ... somebody else will ...

GWEN II. No, Gwen, nobody's gonna come along. Look at yourself ... <u>nobody's</u> gonna come along.

GWEN. ... people still fall in love ... people still fall in love.

GWEN II. But not people like you ... not people like <u>us</u>. *(GWEN slowly raises the gun and points it at GWEN II)* That has no power over me. I'm not flesh and blood. I have no vulnerable heart or brain or finite senses. I don't breathe. I don't sleep. And I don't bleed. <u>You're</u> the only one who's caught in mortality. *(GWEN shoots her)* Now you've only got one bullet left ... don't miss. Embed it in what's left of your brain in such a way that this idiocy finally ends. I'll survive for a short time after you're gone. I'll be the residual, the little bit left behind. I shall speak the last word ... one last murmur

GWEN and GWEN

of something. A name ... what's the last name you want me to say, Gwen? Mother? Mother Earth? What's her name? Mary Lou or Mary Jane or Typhoid Mary, or something like that?

GWEN. *(Stares at the gun)* ... something like that ... don't talk about her.

GWEN II. Fine. How about your old man, huh? What is his name anyway? Has he even got a name?

GWEN. ... no ... he hasn't got a name.

GWEN II. Your damn right he hasn't. All he is is some feeble-minded nonentity who ejaculated one night and, lo and behold, there you were! I guess we can eliminate him. How about ... Kathleen? No? Billie, the Mad Lesbian? Or Estelle, the Handmaiden of the Lord? *(GWEN shakes her head)* How about the fish, Gwen? *(GWEN shakes her head)* How about ... him? How about his name, Gwen?

GWEN. ... how about your name?

GWEN II. *(Startled)* ... my name?

GWEN. Yeah. Have you got a name?

GWEN II. *(Laughs)* Have I got a name?! I've got many names! I am the Nightmare! I am the Sorceress! I am the Jealousy! I am the Story Teller!

GWEN. Say your name! I want to hear you say your name!

GWEN II. I am the Liberator! I am the Fortress! I am the Freedom! I am the Evil Puppet! I am the Dream! I am the Key!

GWEN. You don't remember your name, do you?

GWEN II. I know my name! I know who I am! I am no one!

GWEN. Alright. Then say your childrens' names!

GWEN II. *(Turns away defiantly)* I don't have any children.

GWEN. You are a _woman_ with two children, a son and a daughter!
GWEN II. No! _You've_ got two children! Not _me_!
GWEN. You are a woman with two children and you don't even remember their names, do you? You've forgotten them.

(She tosses the gun on the bed.)

GWEN II. I never forget anything! I am the Memory!
GWEN. Then say their names!
GWEN II. Say them yourself.
GWEN. Come on! You can say them! You _have_ to say them!
GWEN II. I don't _have_ to say anything! I am the Keeper of Secrets. Let me tell you one.
GWEN. There aren't any secrets. I know everything you know.
GWEN II. You don't know anything. If you did, do you think you'd be here now, in this god-forsaken hovel without a friend in the world, drunk, waving a loaded gun around and yelling at _no one_? I'll tell you one of the _many_ things you don't seem to be aware of. Look around you, Gwen. See this place. Does it seem familiar to you somehow? Have you been here before?
GWEN. ... this is my home.
GWEN II. Look again. This is no home. This is the dark side of the moon. This is the place where it is night all the time. This is the void where you are suspended. Do you feel the strings, Gwen? This is where you moan and wail and struggle within those tangled thoughts. Those memories you

GWEN and GWEN

can't bite through. Those twisted iron bars that keep you perpetually locked within the past. This is the prison. This is the place where crazy people go to die.

GWEN. This place has a door.

GWEN II. Ah, an <u>Estellism</u>. I knew one of those would find its way in here. Go ahead. Try the door. It's locked. Locked from the outside.

GWEN. You are the key.

GWEN II. I can't open that door.

GWEN. You opened it once before, remember? The night you came here?

GWEN II. I opened it from the outside. Now we're <u>inside</u> ... trapped.

GWEN. There's windows.

GWEN II. Yes, I know. When God shuts a door, he opens a window. Well, God is not always as accommodating as the philosophers, theologians and social workers tell us he is. These windows are painted shut, Gwen. Even Estelle and her <u>love yourself</u> and her Cape Cod curtains couldn't get us out of here. This is the tomb. *(Points to the door)* On the outside of that door it says, here lies Gwen Kessler, perennial loser, daughter of a zombie and a witch, mother of two abused and abandoned children, and mourned by no one.

GWEN. We can't be dead when there's so much rage. Death is quiet. Death is still. Say your name.

GWEN II. You seem to think that's some sort of magical spell. If I say I am Gwen Kessler, then all will be well again.

GWEN. ... say it.

GWEN II. Very well. I am Gwen Kessler. I just got out of the nut house. My life has been an abysmal failure and I possess no foreseeable future. I am drunk. I am angry. I abused and neglected my children. I have a gun with one bullet in it and I'm thinking of shooting myself, but I'm not dead yet. I am too full of rage. And where there's rage, there's <u>life</u>! There. You got your wish. Are you happy now? Did that change anything?

GWEN. Did it? Go on. Say more.

GWEN II. More? Alright ... I am broke. I hate my parents. I hate myself. I look like shit. The only man I can get is a fat slob who makes me sick. I want to tell my social worker to go fuck herself. And I have two children who I can't support, either financially or emotionally.

GWEN. And their names are?

GWEN II. Sorry, Gweny. That's all I remember about you. That's all there is to remember.

GWEN. I'll give you a clue. Your daughter's name begins with D.

GWEN II. D, huh? How about ... despair? Desertion? Desolation? How about dismemberment? How about ... death?

GWEN. How about ... Diane?

GWEN II. I don't recall anybody by that name.

GWEN. Sure you do. *(Produces the flower drawing from the photo album)* See. She and her brother drew you some flowers. They made this for you when they came to visit you.

GWEN II. *(Stares at the drawing; reaches out to touch it, but then pulls away)* ... nobody ever drew me flowers. And nobody ever came to visit me. No visitors were allowed on the dark side of the moon.

GWEN. Diane did. You were looking at them before. You thought they were pretty.

GWEN. <u>Nothing</u> is <u>pretty</u> in here.

GWEN and GWEN

GWEN. Say your son's name.

GWEN II. *(Sarcastically)* Does that begin with a D, too?

GWEN. You know it does.

GWEN II. Oh, let me see ... Dumpy, Dopey, Dizzy?

GWEN. His name is ... David. Say it. Say David.

GWEN II. Diane and David. My, what nice names for the nicest little kids in the world.

GWEN. Say ... I am Gwen Kessler ... and I have two children ... Diane and David.

GWEN II. I am the daughter of Typhoid Mary and I have two gold fish, Billie and Estelle.

GWEN. I am <u>Gwen Kessler</u> ... and I have two children ... Diane and David.

GWEN II. I am the Nightmare and I have two children. The girl is Dismemberment and her brother is Death. *(Laughs)* I'm only teasing you, Gweny. Okay. I'll say it. I am Gwen Kessler and I have two children ... Diane and David. There! Did your magic spell work? Did you get your grip on reality back? Are the cobwebs and horror all gone now? Will Mother Earth and the feeble old man who sired you walk in here now, embrace you, confirm you, say they love you, and take you to Disneyland? Hell, no! They're the ones who taught you to <u>hate</u> yourself!

GWEN. I don't want to go to Disneyland. All I want ... all I want ...

GWEN II. Careful. You're running out of wishes, Gwen.

GWEN. All I want is for you to come back to me.

GWEN II. That's wish number two and it's a <u>big</u> one, Gweny.

GWEN. And to talk to my children. That's all I want in the world right now.

GWEN II. Wish number three can be easily granted. *(Gestures toward the phone)* There's the phone. Go ahead and call them.

GWEN. If I do ... will you talk to them?

GWEN II. *(Shocked)* Me? Talk to them? You're out of wishes, Gwen. And you're asking for too much. You're asking for healing. You're asking to be a functioning human being like Estelle who flits through life, loving herself. It's too late for us. We learned the other lesson too well. Our teachers were too damn good. And once you learn how to hate ... what's the use, Gwen?

GWEN. I don't hate you.

GWEN II. Maybe not, but I do. And changing hatred into love requires more than the puny little tricks Estelle has up her sleeve. That's merely social worker illusion. We need a miracle. A water-into-wine, parting-of-the-Red-Sea miracle, and I understand that God is rather stingy with miracles in this modern day and age. It's simply not fashionable anymore.

GWEN. *(Picks up the phone, dials, and hands the receiver to GWEN II)* I don't hate you ... and we're still alive. I'd say that's a miracle, wouldn't you?

GWEN II. *(Watches her dial, then grabs the phone away from her)* Don't do it, Gwen!

GWEN. *(Shoves her away)* I'm going to call my children!

GWEN II. Don't do it! They don't love you! You abandoned them! You hit them! You abused them! You left them with your bitch sister and her drunk husband! They hate you!

GWEN. My children do not hate me! They drew me flowers! They do not hate me!

GWEN II. You blamed them! You said it was their fault he left you! You wished they were dead! You wished you never had them!

GWEN. My children love me ... and I'm going to call them.

GWEN II. Estelle would be proud, so proud. Well, go ahead. Call them. They won't even remember who you are. They'll say, we don't have a mother anymore. We had one once, but she lost her mind. What was her name? It began with a G ... let's see ... Gertrude ... Gladys ... Grizzly ... Gruesome ... <u>Gone</u>, something like that.

GWEN. My children remember me ... they've forgiven me ... and they want me back.

GWEN II. *(Phone rings; they both stare at it; GWEN II comes up behind GWEN and frantically grabs her arm)* But what will we say? What will we say? We blamed them! We deserted them! We <u>hurt</u> them! What will we say?!

GWEN. ... we'll say their names.

(Picks up the phone.)

END OF PLAY

COSTUME PLOT

ESTELLE:
Conservative gray business suit, black pumps

MOTHER:
Plain gray house dress, dark sweater, black loafers

GWEN:
(ACT I)
White blouse, dark slacks, wind-breaker jacket, brown loafers
(ACT II)
Drab sweater, dark slacks, brown loafers
(ACT III)
Dark solid color winter jacket, dark slacks, brown loafers

GWEN II:
(ACT I)
Dark formal jumpsuit, mink coat, black heels
(ACT II)
Black jumpsuit, silver jacket, black heels
(ACT III)
Full length black formal dress with slip up side, red satin above-the-elbow gloves, expensive jewelry, black heels

GWEN and GWEN

FURNITURE & PROPERTY LIST

ACT I, Scene One:
(all pieces should be distressed and look as dingy as possible)
   On Stage: bed (R), small kitchen table and 2 chairs (C), sink unit (practical) (UC) (in it - raisins in drawer), old refrigerator (UC), small table (L) (on it - telephone, phone book), chair (L of small table), some trash (spread all over)
   Personal: Estelle: purse (in it - address book)

ACT I, Scene Two:
   Off Stage: grocery sack (in it - wheat thins, Bisquick, etc. & sheets/towels) (Estelle), suitcase (Gwen)
   Personal: Gwen II: purse (in it - pint whiskey bottle, cig. case with cigs, lighter, mirror, hair pick)

ACT II:
   Set: more trash, pop cans, fast food wrappers, etc. (spread all over), on phone table: photo album, kid's flower drawing or watercolor
   Off Stage: cleaning bucket (in it - sponge, rags, power cleaner, etc.) (Mom)

ACT III:
   Set: still more trash (spread all over), on phone table: photo, in sink: 2 drinking glasses, under sink: fancy liquor bottle (half full), in refrigerator: catsup bottle, hidden in bed sheets: revolver with a blank
   Personal: eyebrow pencil (Gwen II)

Note to Designers: All designs should be the image of Gwen's view of "her world": the set should be such a dingy and dark place that no one would even think of living in it. As the play proceeds, Gwen's costumes get progressively more drab and asexual as Gwen II's gets progressively more striking, elegant and flamboyant. Lighting should accent the dim and dingy apartment and may get more bizarre as the play progresses.

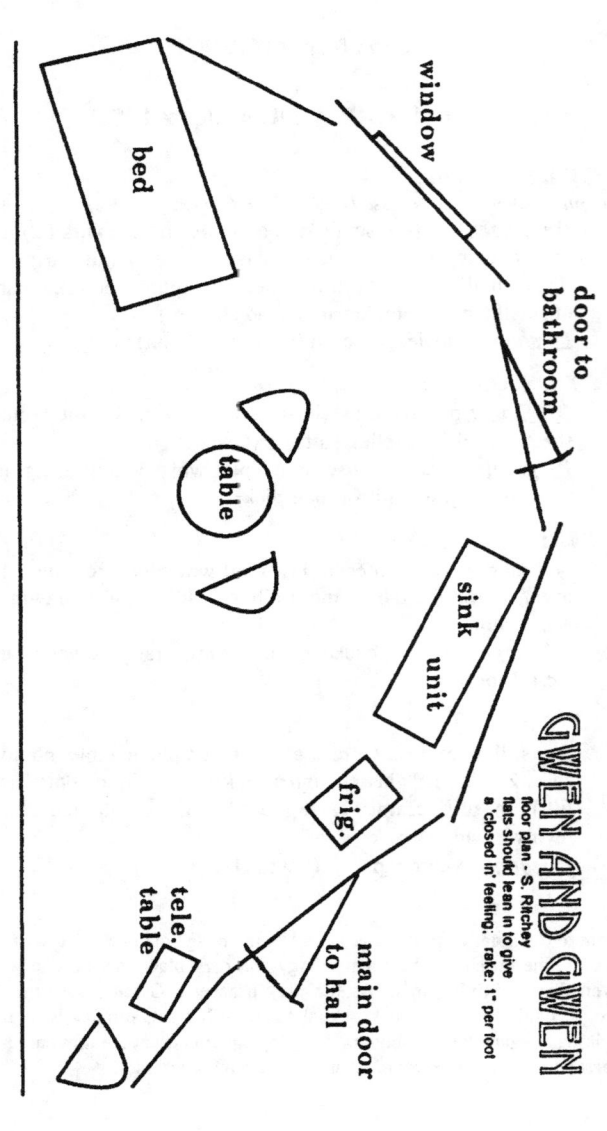

www.ingramcontent.com/pod-product-compliance
Lightning Source LLC
Chambersburg PA
CBHW051409290426
44108CB00015B/2219